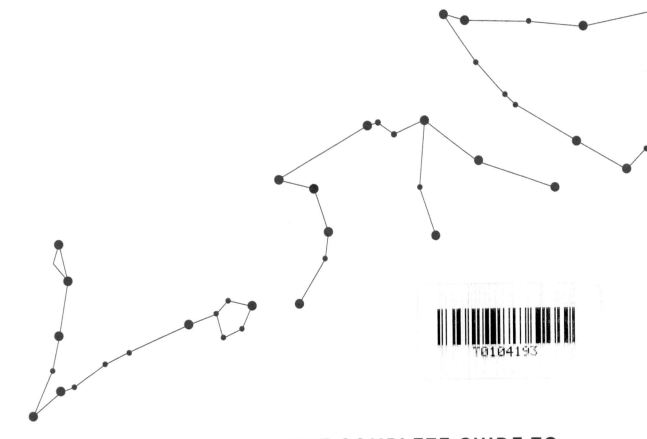

THE COMPLETE GUIDE TO
ASTROLOGY

THE COMPLETE GUIDE TO
ASTROLOGY

UNDERSTANDING YOURSELF, YOUR SIGNS, AND YOUR BIRTH CHART

LOUISE EDINGTON

ROCKRIDGE
PRESS

For general information on our other products and services or to obtain technical support, please contact our Customer Care Department within the United States at (866) 744-2665, or outside the United States at (510) 253-0500.

Rockridge Press publishes its books in a variety of electronic and print formats. Some content that appears in print may not be available in electronic books, and vice versa.

Interior and Cover Designer: Lisa Schreiber
Art Producer: Sara Feinstein
Editor: Lia Ottaviano

Author photo courtesy of © Don Hajicek.

ISBN: Print 978-1-64611-166-4 | eBook 978-1-64611-167-1

R0

I dedicate this book to my friend Karen Krawczyk, who started me on the path of becoming an astrologer in 1989.

CONTENTS

INTRODUCTION

The Complete Guide to Astrology: Understanding Yourself, Your Signs, and Your Birth Chart is written for everyone, from beginner to advanced practitioners and students. In this book, I endeavor to cover a wide range of information in an accessible and inclusive way.

I see the astrological chart as a blueprint of potential and possibility. You will never find me saying that any sign or placement is all good or all bad, and I believe that it is always possible to find a way through any challenges or blocks to growth, evolution, and compatibility. This book is written from that approach. We are nuanced and we all have the ability to consciously approach how we navigate our cosmic blueprint. That said, I do not use spiritual override—that is, use spiritual practices to sidestep unresolved issues or wounds—as I prefer to take a firm look at the shadow and how that shadow can be healed or integrated rather than bypassed.

I now invite you to look at the subject of gender differently. Astrological language has traditionally been binary, using male and female and masculine and feminine labels. Yet our astrological chart, or cosmic blueprint, contains every planet and sign, and therefore, they are all within each of us. The astrological chart does not show gender, so neither does this book. I focus on the whole person and their characteristics, removing binary identifiers entirely. The content of this book will give you a thorough grounding in key foundational areas of astrology and takes a radically different approach to astrological language as we come to understand that the planetary bodies and signs are innately nonbinary in nature.

Throughout this book I integrate the terms "day" and "night" to replace masculine/male and feminine/female respectively, as the two terms are less limiting. This is a concept that was used by the ancients and that loosely aligned with masculine and feminine for them. I will say more on this in chapter 1. I would like to thank astrologer Jason Holley for introducing me to this concept and the work of Robert Hand and Brian Clark for helping me expand upon it.

The concepts of day and night allow us to take a more humanistic approach to the inner landscape of the soul. Therefore, although this book is partly an instruction manual to help you interpret your chart, it's also asking you to take a more radical and nonbinary approach to the language of astrology.

I have always loved astrology. I still have things I wrote as young teen delineating sun-sign qualities. It wasn't until my first Saturn return at age 29 (when Saturn returns to the position it was at in one's natal chart) that I discovered what I then called "real" astrology. A friend read my chart for me and gave me some books and I was hooked. That was in 1989.

I devoured those books, taught myself how to hand-draw natal charts, bought and devoured more books, subscribed to magazines, and practiced on my friends and their children. I then got married and had children and my astrological intensity faded for a few years, though I never lost my fascination with astrology.

By October 2012, I had moved continents twice (from the United Kingdom to Australia to the United States), my children were 15 and 13, and I was working in the coaching world when I had a revelation that my purpose was to work as a professional astrologer. I worked with a teacher one-on-one and took other classes to hone the art, and within a few months I began to work professionally as an astrologer. I still take classes today, because astrology is a glorious and never-ending rabbit hole where there is always more to discover.

I have now done thousands of readings, run classes, and written astrology articles almost daily. In November 2018, I published my first book, *Modern Astrology: Harness the Stars to Discover Your Soul's True Purpose*, which I wrote as a tool for personal growth. I am also a shamanic practitioner and an activist.

I am a Sagittarius sun with a Sagittarius stellium in the 11th and 12th houses, Sagittarius rising, and a Gemini moon. For those of you who already understand the basics of astrology, that will tell you that I am a writer, a teacher, and attracted to social and political justice, which I cannot help but bring into my work.

This book is written for those who wish to take their astrological study to another level and to do so from a place of inclusivity. This book is for everyone. Welcome.

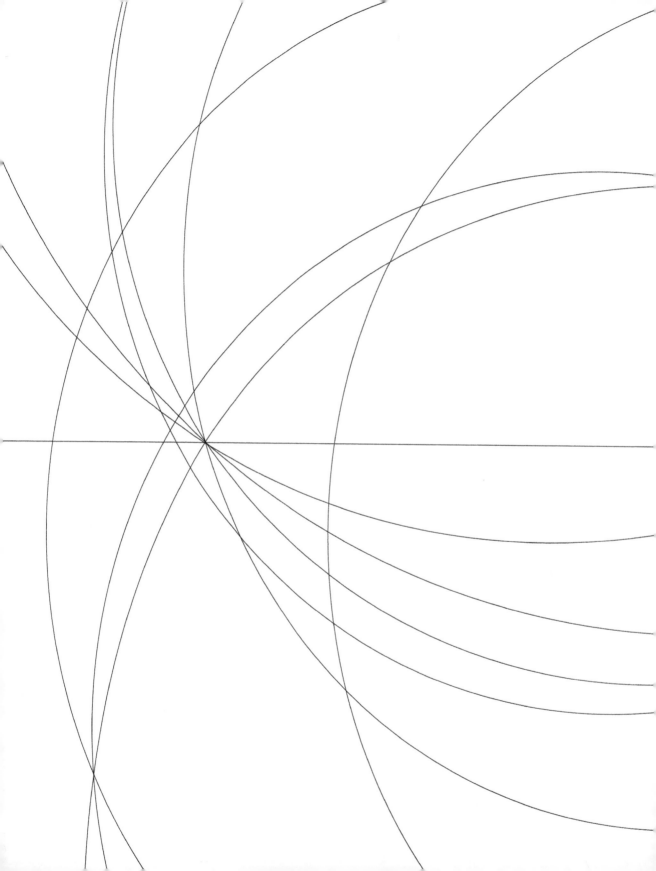

THE BUILDING BLOCKS OF
ASTROLOGY

IN PART 1, we'll be taking a brief look at the history of astrology, where astrology is today, and how to look at the language of astrology in a new way. We'll also be covering some of the basic building blocks of the astrological chart and how you can start to interpret yours.

PART

1

An Astrological Foundation

FOR MILLENNIA, ASTROLOGY has been used to predict events. More recently, people have begun using astrology as a tool for personal development and growth, seeking insight into their personal patterns, limiting beliefs, and potential.

Astrology can help us live in alignment with the elements and cycles of nature, choose optimum timing for everything from farming to relationships to work life, and engage in psychological exploration and past life lessons. Astrology can help us heal our disconnection with the natural cycles of the universe and live in harmony with the cosmic cycles as they work within us.

At its highest level, astrology is a tool that brings each of us into a higher spiritual connection with the universe and the cycles of the universe, helping us make conscious choices to live up to our highest potential. My approach to consciousness is humanistic and psychological, and the inner landscape is my focus. We each have every planet and sign working within our soul consciousness. The language of astrology has inadequately expressed that up until now. Times are changing, and so must the language of astrology.

Why does astrology work? That's an eternal question, but my response is that it's based on thousands of years of observation. Even though it has been through periods of decline, humanity has always returned to the study of astrology, because skilled interpretation of the movements of the cosmos provides answers to the meaning and cycles of life.

WHAT IS ASTROLOGY?

Astrology is an ancient science that uses observation of the planetary cycles and movements over time to record patterns and events triggered by the movement of the cosmos.

As the Moon's cycles so clearly affect the Earth's tides, menstrual and other biorhythmic cycles, and our emotional energies, the other cosmic bodies, luminaries, planets, asteroids, and beyond work within us as well. Everything in the universe is connected, a fact long known by astrologers but now being recognized by scientists using quantum mechanics, which suggests that every atom affects other atoms. In quantum physics, everything is made of waves and particles and works according to entanglement theory, which suggests that no particle is entirely independent. In a nutshell, everything in the universe works together and the movements of the cosmic bodies activate energy within us and the natural world. In other words, we are entangled with the entire universe. All the energies intertwine in an intricate dance of planetary magic and science, and the language of astrology interprets that dance.

The roots of astrology go back thousands of years. Archaeologists have found evidence that humans may have tracked lunar cycles from the earliest of times, such as cave paintings marked with lunar cycles. Some of this evidence may date back as far as 30,000 BCE.

Astrology is often said to be based on calendrical systems, but I would suggest that calendrical systems are based on the movement of the cosmic bodies—the earliest calendars were based on the movement of the Sun, the star Sirius (Egyptian calendar), or the Moon (Greek calendar).

In other words, witnessing and recording the planetary cycles came first, and then calendrical systems came from the movement of the cosmos. This means that astrology is at the root of all our lives.

Astrology has evolved over thousands of years and there are several different astrological disciplines, including but not limited to Vedic (Jyotish Vidya or Hindi) astrology, which is based on the sidereal zodiac rather than the tropical zodiac used by western astrology; Chinese astrology, which is based on a 12-year cycle; Hellenistic astrology, which is a Greco-Roman tradition practiced from the first century BCE until the seventh century CE and currently experiencing a revival; and modern western astrology, which is my own practice and is based on the tropical zodiac. Western astrology originated from Ptolemaic and Babylonian astrology, which takes a more psychological and developmental approach.

Key figures in astrological history include Ptolemy (second century CE), who wrote one of the key astrological texts, the *Tetrabiblos*; Carl Jung (1875–1961), who was a pioneer in using astrology in the field of psychology; Alan Leo (1860–1917), often called the father of modern astrology; and one of my personal favorites, Dane Rudhyar (1895–1985), who coined the term "humanistic astrology" and helped pioneer modern astrological practices.

This book is based on the modern western tradition. However, all traditions have validity and only differ in their approach—some being more predictive, such as Vedic, and some taking a more personal growth or psychological approach.

Modern western astrology is centered on creating a chart or horoscope that is cast for a specific time, date, and place using the tropical zodiac, which is based on the symbolic relationship between the Earth and the Sun. The tropical zodiac divides the ecliptic into 12 equal parts of 30° each (the signs) and is oriented to the seasons, with the zodiac beginning on the vernal equinox, when the Sun moves into Aries. The ecliptic is an imaginary line, or plane, in the sky that marks the apparent annual path of the sun along which eclipses occur.

ASTROLOGY'S HISTORICAL ORIGINS

Apart from the early evidence of the tracking of lunar cycles in cave paintings and on bones, the recorded history of astrology really began with the Sumerians in Mesopotamia 6,000 years ago, who noted the movements of the cosmos, as well as Vedic or Jyotish astrology, which began at least 5,000 years ago in India.

From around 2,400 to 331 BCE, the Babylonians, also known as the Chaldeans, created the zodiac wheel with planets, the 12 houses representing areas of life and development.

After Alexander the Great conquered the Babylonians, the Greeks further developed astrology, giving the planets and zodiac signs their modern names. In 140 CE, Ptolemy published *Tetrabiblos,* which contained planets, houses, aspects, and angles, all techniques astrologers still use to this day.

Over the centuries, the study and use of astrology waxed and waned in the west, but it flourished in the Middle Ages, when it was a part of mathematics, astronomy, and the medical world. There were royal astrologers, and the oldest universities had astrology chairs.

As the church gained power, astrology began to decline. The Age of Reason, including the Protestant reform movement in the 17th and 18th centuries, began to promote reason and skepticism over what came to be seen as entertainment only. Astrology, therefore, lost popularity until its resurgence in the late 19th century.

ASTROLOGY TODAY

Western astrology as we know it today began its resurgence in the late 19th century. Alan Leo is generally credited with the beginning of the renewed interest in astrology and the development of a more spiritual and esoteric approach as a theosophist. Theosophy is a teaching about God and the world based on mystical insights. Alan Leo introduced the concepts of karma and reincarnation into his work as an astrologer and began the move away from event-oriented astrology into character analysis.

Another theosophist, Dane Rudhyar, was also involved in this resurgence. He really began the psychological approach to astrology and coined the term "humanistic astrology." Rudhyar's work was based on theosophy and eastern philosophies primarily, and he was influenced by the psychology of Carl Jung. Rudhyar's work is the basis of much of the modern astrology developed in the 1960s and 1970s.

Most modern western astrology is focused on the psychological and humanistic side, though there is currently a resurgence in some more ancient and predictive techniques, especially among younger astrologers.

The gender assignments of planets and signs are problematic in the modern

Famous Astrology Followers

Throughout history, astrology has been popular with leaders, rulers, and other famous people. Catholic popes were interested in astrology in the Middle Ages and relied on the predictions and advice of astrologers for the timing of coronations and to help them make important decisions.

A college for astrologers was founded in Paris by Charles V, Catherine de Médicis was known to consult with Nostradamus, and Ronald and Nancy Reagan regularly consulted with astrologers.

J. P. Morgan was one of many business leaders who consulted astrology before making business decisions and once said in a court deposition, "Millionaires don't have astrologers, billionaires do." Additionally, former U.S. Secretary of the Treasury Donald Regan once said, "It's common knowledge that a large percentage of Wall Street brokers use astrology." Other celebrities and well-known people who are known to have consulted with astrologers include Lady Gaga, Madonna, Albert Einstein, and Theodore Roosevelt.

world. The feminine has primarily been designated as passive, receptive, weak, dark, and destructive, whereas the masculine has been designated as powerful, action-oriented, light, positive, and dominant—and there has been no consideration of other genders. The planet names are based on the Roman and Greek pantheons, which were firmly patriarchal in nature. Only the Moon and Venus of the main essential bodies were designated as feminine. This isn't true of many older cultures, where the planets were seen differently. For example, there were many Sun goddesses in ancient cultures, and the Moon was often seen as the sperm to the Sun's ovum. In this book, I am moving away from these binary definitions, as we are all the Sun and the Moon and other planetary bodies, and each cosmic body has both strengths and weaknesses that are not gender-specific.

Here, we'll be integrating, and expanding on, the theory of an old Hellenistic technique called sects, which defined planets as diurnal (of the day) and nocturnal (of the night). In this system, the Sun, Jupiter, and Saturn were diurnal, and Venus, Mars, and the Moon were nocturnal. Mercury bridged the gap. In the vein of some current astrologers working to create a more inclusive and nonbinary approach to astrological language, we'll be using the words "day" and "night." These delineations make sense, as day and night are visible—day is more "yang," or outward oriented, and night is more "yin," or inward oriented. As the planetary table in the astrological tables section shows clearly, the five personal planets—Mercury, Venus, Mars, Jupiter, and Saturn—all have both day and night qualities depending on the energy of the sign of traditional rulership. This adds a deeper interpretation, moving us away from the inherently patriarchal and binary language of astrology that has been used until now.

The solar system is a living, breathing, and pulsing organism that inhales (diurnal) and exhales (nocturnal), with all planetary bodies, signs, houses, and aspects having either day/inhale energy or night/exhale energy—sometimes both. I associate day with the energy of the inhalation, because we inhale the breath of life to give ourselves the outgoing energy for the day. At night we release or exhale to recharge. This reflects the quantum entanglement of the solar system within each living organism—and within each of us.

CHAPTER TWO

The Four Elements and Three Modalities

IN THIS CHAPTER, I will be exploring the three modalities—cardinal, fixed, and mutable—and the four key elements— fire, earth, air, and water. Modalities are also known as the qualities of the signs, or their basic modus operandi—the way they work. Each of the three modalities includes four astrological signs, one from each of the elements. The four elements each represent one characteristic: Fire represents spirit, water represents emotion, air represents intellect, and earth represents the physical.

The zodiac, like the universe itself, is composed of these four elements, and in astrology, they represent archetypal characteristics within a person. As the luminaries, planets, asteroids, and other cosmic bodies work in alignment within us, so too do the elements. The elements also work in harmony with each other, so please be aware that every element is contained within each person.

Each element is connected to three signs of the zodiac and the predominant element in a horoscope gives a clear indication of how a person reacts, responds, and behaves. An analysis of the elemental balance alone in the chart can say a lot about the primary traits of a person.

The four elements are further divided into the three modalities as follows:

Aries is Cardinal Fire
Taurus is Fixed Earth
Gemini is Mutable Air
Cancer is Cardinal Water

Leo is Fixed Fire
Virgo is Mutable Earth
Libra is Cardinal Air
Scorpio is Fixed Water

Sagittarius is Mutable Fire
Capricorn is Cardinal Earth
Aquarius is Fixed Air
Pisces is Mutable Water

Blending the elements with the modalities gives us even more information about the primary traits of a person. For example, Gemini is mutable air and is, therefore, more likely to be very changeable; Libra is cardinal air and more likely to initiate new ideas.

CARDINAL MODALITY

The first of the three modalities is the cardinal modality, which is associated with the four signs that begin each quadrant of the natural zodiac: Aries, Cancer, Libra, and Capricorn. Aries and Libra are the day (or inhale) cardinal signs and Cancer and Capricorn are the night (or exhale) signs.

As modalities represent the basic mode of operation of a sign, all four cardinal signs are initiating energies that begin a new season or stage of life and this, therefore, is reflected in their nature. Cardinal signs like to begin new projects. They are the pioneers of the zodiac but may lack the staying power needed to bring ideas and projects to fruition.

FIXED MODALITY

The second of the three modalities is the fixed modality, which is associated with the four signs that are in the middle of each quadrant of the natural zodiac:

Taurus, Leo, Scorpio, and Aquarius. Here we also have two night (or exhale) signs, Taurus and Scorpio, and two day (or inhale) signs, Leo and Aquarius.

The fixed signs do exactly what they say they will. Their basic way of behaving is to fix in place that which was initiated by the cardinal signs. They have the staying power to make the projects, plans, and ideas of the cardinal, or initiating, signs happen. Fixed signs generally like continuity and dislike change. But life and the universe are ever-moving, which brings us to the third modality.

MUTABLE MODALITY

The third of the three modalities is the mutable modality, which is associated with the four signs that end each quadrant of the natural zodiac and that lead into the beginning of the next: Gemini, Virgo, Sagittarius, and Pisces. Gemini and Sagittarius are the day (or inhale) signs and Virgo and Pisces are the night (or exhale) signs.

As their name suggests, mutable signs are very flexible, changeable, and versatile. They can usually see all sides of issues and cope well when life throws change at them. They can, however, easily lose focus and purpose in life and are likely to suffer from "shiny object syndrome" and distraction.

The Horoscope as the Medicine Wheel

The four elements and the four signs of the cardinal modality have also been used in shamanic cultures for millennia as the medicine wheel, which represents the four cardinal directions called in ceremony and the beginning of the seasons. In the northern hemisphere, cardinal Aries (fire) begins spring, cardinal Cancer (water) begins summer, cardinal Libra (air) begins fall, and cardinal Capricorn (earth) begins winter. These are reversed in the southern hemisphere.

The four directions also represent stages of life: birth (east, fire, new beginnings), youth (south, water, emotional innocence and trust), adulthood (west, earth, physical energy), and elderhood (north, air, wisdom). The whole horoscope could therefore be seen as a medicine wheel or sacred hoop of life to align with. Please note that this is one way of looking at this and different shamanic traditions look at the wheel of life differently.

The seasons of the year align with the seasons of life through birth (Spring), youth (Summer), adulthood (Fall), and elderhood (Winter). Everything is connected in a great mandala of creation.

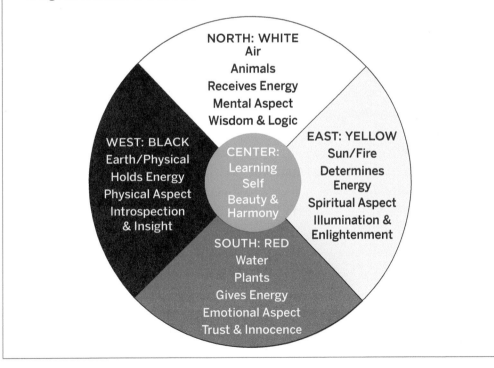

FIRE 🔥

Fire is the energy of transformation and action and is day (inhale) energy. As we inhale life, we draw breath to gain energy. We also expand our lungs on inhalation; fire signs and planets are expansive or outgoing. Fire is heat and movement. Think about the energy of flames, as you watch them flicker and dance, and you get a feeling for the element of fire. The Sun provides the Earth and humanity with the heat and light we need to survive.

Fire is fast-moving and transformative, like a phoenix rising from the ashes of destruction.

The three fire signs—Aries, Leo, and Sagittarius—are positive, inspirational, enthusiastic, and confident. They are more associated with day energy, which is more direct and focused outward but all signs have some fire energy contained within, as we are all elements in differing quantities.

Aries, ruled by the warrior god Mars, is the first of the fire signs and is the most direct and focused. Leo, ruled by the Sun, is confident and loves attention. Sagittarius, ruled by Jupiter, is expansive and inspirational.

Any placements, luminaries, planets, asteroids, or angles in fire signs will take on these characteristics. For example, those with Venus (values and love) in Aries are very direct and more warrior-like in relationships. People with Mercury (the mind and communication) in Leo have a communication style that conveys authority.

WATER 〰️

Water is the energy of receptivity and emotion and is a night (exhale) energy. Water, like emotions, is fluid and shifting. Water makes up a huge percentage of the human body and could be said to be the most crucial element. Cancer, Scorpio, and Pisces are the three water signs; all are deeply intuitive and creative energies.

The Moon rules Cancer and is associated with nurturing and mothering. Pluto rules Scorpio, which reflects the depth of this sign and is associated with obsession and psychological depths. Neptune rules Pisces and is associated with all meditative or altered states, as well as the connection to the collective unconscious or spirit energy.

Any placements in water signs take on a more fluid energy. Someone with Mercury (the mind and communication) in Cancer, for example, receives information instinctively and retains it at a deep level, since Cancer is a receptive night energy.

AIR △

Air is the energy of the mind or thought and is a day (inhale) energy. This is the breath and the wind. We can't hold on to breath; it flows in and out, and wind is needed to stop the air around us from becoming stagnant. Gemini, Libra, and Aquarius are the three air signs, and they are the signs of thought, ideas, sociability, and the analytical. Air signs are associated with rationality and the right brain.

Gemini, ruled by Mercury, is associated with duality and learning. Libra, ruled by Venus, is associated with diplomacy, relationships, and mediation. Aquarius is ruled by Uranus and is associated with the Internet because of its connectivity of thoughts, ideas, and people; higher intellect; inventiveness; and innovation.

Any placements in air signs take on an airier flavor. Someone with Mars (drive and will) in Gemini, for example, is a fast learner and likely to speak very quickly and directly.

EARTH ▽

Earth is the energy of the material world, energy that you can touch and feel. Earth is stable, practical, and patient, and it is a night (exhale) energy. Taurus, Virgo, and Capricorn are the three earth signs, and they are the signs of hard work, building, creating material things, and connection to the material world and structures.

Earth signs are sensual, have creative qualities, and are connected to the natural cycles of nature, as well as the human cycle of birth, life, and death.

Taurus, ruled by Venus, is the most connected with the material world and the Earth itself. Virgo, ruled by Mercury, is more connected with the technical world and crafts. Capricorn, ruled by Saturn, is the pioneer of the earth signs and is the leadership and achievement-oriented sign.

Any placements in earth signs will take on the flavor of the sign. For example, someone with Mars (drive and will) in Taurus will be slower and more deliberate than someone with Mars in the sign of rulership, Aries, which is very fast-moving and direct.

CHAPTER THREE

The Sun Signs ☉

IN THIS CHAPTER, I will be discussing the 12 sun signs of the zodiac. In contemporary astrology, the sun signs represent our core self and could be said to represent our ego. The sun signs are the part of the self that almost everyone knows and the primary energy that fuels our being. I will provide keywords, technical details—such as ruling planet—and some fun facts about each sign. We'll be looking at dualities (night/feminine/yin or day/masculine/yang) in this section. View the signs as an evolution of personal development from birth, Aries, to end of life, Pisces, so that you gain a deeper understanding of how the signs work within you—we all have energy from every sign within us, no matter what our sun sign is.

ARIES ♈

Aries is the first sign of the zodiac and is seen by most to be the start of the astrological year—the ingress (or moving into) of the Sun into Aries signals the spring equinox in the northern hemisphere and Aries is the first sign in the natural horoscope, ruling the first house.

The sign spans the first 30° of the zodiac and the Sun transits the sign from the equinox, approximately March 21 to April 20. These dates change according to the Sun's actual movement in the sky from our perspective here on Earth.

Aries is a day cardinal fire sign, is ruled by Mars, the god of war, and represents youth, which is very focused on the self. The Aries symbol is the ram, and its glyph represents the horns of the ram. Aries is in polarity with the sign of Libra, an air sign, which means they are complementary and work well together. The dominant keyword for Aries is "**I am**," which means they are all about the self and like to come first. Aries rules the head and eyes. Red is the color associated with Aries, diamond is the birthstone, and iron is the metal.

The most likeable traits for Aries are that they are dynamic, pioneering, and seen as leaders by others. Inwardly, they have a healthy self-interest and are very courageous. They may have a tendency to be aggressive and reactionary if their directness isn't tempered. Others see Aries as impatient, fast-moving, and daring.

Lady Gaga, Elton John, Nancy Pelosi, and Leonardo da Vinci were all born under the sign of Aries.

TAURUS ♉

The second sign of the zodiac is Taurus. The Sun transits this sign from about April 21 to May 20, and it rules the second house.

Taurus is a night fixed earth sign and is ruled by Venus in her material world incarnation as goddess of the manifest. Like Aries, this sign is represented by a horned animal, the bull, indicating that these first two signs are very straightforward and "headfirst." The glyph for Taurus represents the head and horns of the bull. Taurus represents the stage of life that realizes the connection with the physical world.

Scorpio is the sign that is in polarity to Taurus, and the two complement each other well. Like the strong and solid bull that represents the sign, the dominant keyword for Taurus is "**build**," as the those born under the sign love to develop all that endures. The sign of Taurus is

associated with the throat and vocal cords, the gemstone most associated with the sign is emerald—but being the most material of signs, Taurus is also associated with sapphires—and copper is the metal.

Taurus embodies animal wisdom in that they have finely honed senses and are sensual, practical, and loyal. Inwardly, they are deeply grounded, patient, and steady, but this can also lead to the tendency to be stubborn or bullheaded and overly materialistic in the pursuit of security. Others see Taurus as stable and lacking in pretense.

Queen Elizabeth II, Mark Zuckerberg, and Dwayne "The Rock" Johnson were born under the sign of Taurus. (The nickname "The Rock" really is emblematic of the sign, as rocks are of the earth element.)

GEMINI ♊

Gemini spans the third 30° of the zodiac. The Sun transits this sign from about May 21 to June 20, and Gemini rules the third house of the zodiac.

Gemini is a day mutable air sign and is one of two signs ruled by Mercury in his mind/messenger incarnation. This sign symbolizes the twins and is represented by a glyph of twins that are both separate and connected. Gemini represents the stage of life when we begin to communicate verbally and to realize both our connection to and our separation from each other.

Sagittarius is the sign that is in polarity to Gemini. Just as Gemini is the sign of the twins, there are a few gemstones said to be lucky for the sign. Yellow stones are most often seen as lucky, such as agate, citrine, and amber. It's no surprise that Gemini's lucky metal is mercury itself. Gemini is associated with the chest, lungs, nervous system, arms, and shoulders.

Gemini is the **thinker** and symbolizes the mind, voice, and communication. Their inner life is curious, observant,

often scattered, and may be highly strung. Geminis are seen as social and verbally expressive but sometimes manipulative and duplicitous.

John F. Kennedy, Donald Trump, Paul McCartney, Prince, and Bob Dylan were all born under the sign of Gemini.

CANCER ♋

Cancer is the fourth sign of the zodiac. From about June 21 to July 20, the Sun transits the sign of Cancer.

Cancer is a night cardinal water sign. The sign is represented by the crab and its glyph is the two pincers of the crab in

Popular Astrology Forecasts

Astrological forecasts that appear on online sites and in magazines and newspapers are the analysis of the chart for each of the signs as a whole and are general in nature. They do, however, have validity, especially if you know your rising sign and can read the forecast for that sign as well as the sun sign.

These forecasts, when done well, will look at the primary transits of the planets currently and how they affect each astrological house after placing the sun sign on the cusp of the first house in a chart for the current time.

For example, if Pluto is in Capricorn by transit and being activated by other transits, and you have a Libra sun, then the forecast will be based on a chart with your Libra sun on the first house cusp. This chart will then show Pluto transiting in your third house, as Capricorn is the third sign after Libra. This may not be your actual third house in your natal chart but will still have some resonance.

If you are Libra rising, then the forecast will be speaking generally about the areas of life contained by your own third house. If you like to read general forecasts, knowing your ascendant will be beneficial.

protective mode. This already says a lot about the energy of the sign of Cancer, as Cancers are primarily introverted and protective. The polarity to Cancer is the earth sign of Capricorn. The lucky metal and gemstones associated with the sign are reflective of its ruler, the Moon: The metal is silver, and the stones are moonstone, pearl, and white quartz. Cancer is associated with the stomach, chest, and breast.

"**Feel**" is the primary word for this sign and Cancers are all emotion and intuition. Cancer is the nurturer of the zodiac and very tradition- and family-oriented. Inwardly, the sign is extremely sensitive and can tend toward being insecure and giving too much, to the point of ignoring their own needs. Others see them as responsive and loving, but they can also be moody.

Princess Diana, the Dalai Lama, Tom Cruise, and Meryl Streep were all born under the sign of Cancer.

LEO ♌

The fifth sign of the zodiac is Leo. The Sun transits the sign of Leo from around July 21 to August 20.

Leo is a day fixed fire sign and is ruled by the Sun. The lion is the symbol of this regal sign and its glyph represents the lion's head and mane. The sign of polarity is Aquarius. Unsurprisingly, gold is the metal associated with Leo and the lucky gemstones are golden and amber colors, such as amber, tiger's eye, and yellow topaz. Leo rules the heart, spine, and upper back.

Leos are born to **lead**, and that is their primary word. Whether king, queen, or leader in their own home, Leos are born to shine and charm. They crave attention and tend to be melodramatic and superior when in shadow. Otherwise, Leos are dynamic, self-confident, and playful. At their best, they are magnetic and affectionate and light up the lives of those around them because they carry the Sun's radiance within.

Barack Obama, Bill Clinton, Madonna, and James Baldwin were all born under the sign of Leo.

VIRGO ♍

The sixth sign of the zodiac is Virgo. The Sun transits the sign of Virgo from around August 21 to September 20.

Virgo is a night mutable earth sign, the second sign to be ruled by Mercury, but in a more technical, detail-oriented, hands-on incarnation. This sign is represented by the maiden or virgin, meaning in this case, "one who is whole unto herself." Its glyph resembles the letter M, for "maiden," carrying a shaft of wheat to represent the harvest. This suggests a state of being that reflects the energies of Virgo, rather than merely a gender. Pisces is the sign in polarity to Virgo. Like Gemini, the other Mercury-ruled sign, Virgo's metal is mercury itself and the lucky gemstones associated with the sign are sapphire, jade, and jasper. The digestive system and spleen are associated with Virgo.

Virgo energy embodies the principle of service, as they love to feel useful in the world. Virgos are attentive to detail and very analytical. Their inner world is often self-critical and they are worriers. They can tend to servitude rather than service and forget to take care of themselves in the process. Others see Virgos as ethical and organized, though I find it to be somewhat of a myth that Virgos are always tidy. This is, in part, because their perfectionist tendencies can lead to analysis paralysis. "**Analyze**" is the primary word for Virgo.

Prince Harry, Mother Teresa, Bernie Sanders, and Freddie Mercury of Queen were all born under the sign of Virgo.

LIBRA ♎

Libra is the seventh sign of the zodiac. Libra season has the Sun transiting the sign from around September 21 to October 20.

Libra is a day cardinal air sign. Libra is ruled by Venus in her more cerebral incarnation. The symbol of Libra is the scales and its glyph reflects both balance and the setting sun as we enter autumn in the northern hemisphere (or the rising sun in the southern hemisphere). Aries is the sign of polarity. Peridot and topaz are Libra's lucky gemstones and the associated metal is copper. The kidneys, skin, lower back, and buttocks are ruled by Libra.

"**Balance**" is the primary word for Libras, because they try to find the middle ground and harmonious balance in all that they do. Libra is the diplomat and mediator of the zodiac. Because of that, they can come across as indecisive, vacillating, and even passive-aggressive at times. Generally, Libra comes across as fair, peace-loving, and creative. Inwardly, they are focused on others and relationships.

Examples of well-known Librans are Mahatma Gandhi, Serena Williams, Will Smith, and Oscar Wilde.

SCORPIO ♏

Ruling the eighth house and, therefore, the eighth sign is Scorpio. The Sun transits the sign of Scorpio from around October 21 to November 20.

Scorpio is a night fixed water sign ruled by Pluto (modern) and Mars (traditional). A deep and complex sign, both its symbol and its glyph represent the scorpion, its stinger suggesting the potentially stinging nature of Scorpio. As a highly complex and transformational sign, however, Scorpio is also associated with the serpent, a symbol of transformation, and the phoenix, a symbol of rebirth. Taurus is the sign of polarity. Iron and steel are associated with Scorpio and ruby and garnet are the lucky gemstones. Scorpio rules the reproductive system and sexual organs.

"**Desire**" is the primary word for the sign of Scorpio, as it reflects the emotional depth and complexity of this magnetic and private sign. Scorpio is seen as magnetic, powerful, and sometimes intimidating by others. Internally, they can be brooding and obsessive but also deeply instinctual and psychological. When Scorpios are able to dive into the most emotionally intense issues of life, they are able to connect with their true power.

Different Uses for Astrology

Although this book deals with natal astrology, it's important to note that astrology has many uses that can be explored both separately and in conjunction with the natal chart.

MUNDANE ASTROLOGY is the astrology of events, organizations, elections, countries, and weather events. The word "mundane" is from the Latin *mundanus*, meaning "worldly." Any event or organization has an inception chart, which is read in a similar way to the natal chart.

FINANCIAL ASTROLOGY is a specialty that predicts financial events and cycles.

HORARY ASTROLOGY is a tool used to answer a specific question based on the time the question is posed. This technique is used for anything where a question can be asked, such as "Where are my keys?"

MEDICAL ASTROLOGY is used to diagnose and treat illness and can also be used for prevention, as it can show areas of weakness in a person's health.

ASTROCARTOGRAPHY, OR LOCATIONAL ASTROLOGY, is based on planetary lines drawn around the globe to indicate how a facet of a person's life is either enhanced or diminished by living in a specific place.

Pablo Picasso, Hedy Lamarr, RuPaul, Leonardo DiCaprio, Lisa Bonet, and John Gotti were all born under the sign of Scorpio.

SAGITTARIUS ♐

The sign ruling the ninth house is Sagittarius. The Sun transits the sign from around November 21 to December 20.

Sagittarius is a day mutable fire sign ruled by Jupiter. The glyph for Sagittarius is an arrow pointing to the stars and reflects the symbol of the archer, who is half-human and half-horse. Both the glyph and symbol reflect the forward-thinking visionary energy of the sign. Gemini is the sign in polarity. Sagittarius rules the hips, thighs, and liver. Turquoise and amethyst are the lucky stones for Sagittarius, and the metal is tin.

"**Wander**" and "**wonder**" are the primary words for Sagittarius, because they like to wander—physically and mentally—and they often live in a state of wonder at the world. Sagittarius is the seeker of truth and freedom and loves exploration of all kinds. They are often seen as naive, inspirational, and eternal optimists. Spiritually oriented and visionary, they have the ability to see the big picture of life. If Sagittarius embraces life as a quest for experience and truth, their tendency toward naïveté can become higher wisdom.

Walt Disney, Jane Fonda, Jimi Hendrix, Jay-Z, and Gianni Versace were all born under the sign of Sagittarius.

CAPRICORN ♑

The 10th sign of the zodiac is Capricorn, and it is ruled by Saturn. The Sun transits the sign of Capricorn from around December 21 to January 20.

Capricorn is a night cardinal earth sign. The symbol for Capricorn is the sea goat, and the glyph represents the hoof of the goat with the tail of a fish—this softer side of Capricorn has been lost in many astrological texts. The polarity of the sign is Cancer. Capricorn rules the skeletal system, teeth, and joints. Capricorn's metal is lead and the gemstone is ruby.

The primary word for Capricorn is "**achieve**." Capricorns are focused on climbing the ladder of achievement but may have a tendency to do so based on the expectations of the outer world rather than based on a foundation of self-trust, which is where the tail of the fish comes in. Capricorn is seen as responsible and determined but also, at times, controlling and fearful. Inwardly, although Capricorn is hardworking and law-abiding, there is often an underlying fear of never being enough. Their commitment and leadership qualities are their strengths.

Jeff Bezos, Elvis Presley, Michelle Obama, and Betty White were all born under the sign of Capricorn.

AQUARIUS ♒

Ruling the 11th house of the zodiac is Aquarius. The Sun transits the sign of Aquarius from around January 21 to February 20.

Aquarius is a day fixed air sign and is ruled by Uranus (modern) and Saturn (traditional). Although the symbol for Aquarius is the water bearer, what the glyph actually represents is waves of energy—the symbol is pouring spirit or energy down from the heavens. This indicates the otherworldly quality of the sign. The polarity of this sign is Leo. The sign's associated metal is lead and the gemstones are obsidian and sapphire. Aquarius rules the calves, ankles, and nervous system.

Aquarians are the individuals of the zodiac and their primary word is "**know**." Aquarians are sometimes seen as the weirdos of the zodiac, as they are unpredictable, inventive, and original in nature. Aquarians are socially conscious and are dedicated to causes and reform, but they can also be emotionally distant and even anarchistic at times. Because they often feel alienated from those around them, they are sometimes tempted to betray their convictions to fit in, but their path is to embody their personal truth no matter what.

Oprah Winfrey, Bob Marley, Ellen DeGeneres, and Franklin D. Roosevelt were all born under the sign of Aquarius.

PISCES ♓

The 12th and final sign of the zodiac is Pisces. From around February 21 to March 20, the Sun transits the sign of Pisces.

Pisces is a night mutable water sign. The symbol for Pisces is the fish and its glyph represents two fish swimming in different directions yet connected by a cord. If we look at the zodiac as a path of human development, Pisces is the time of death and the time before birth, the amniotic fluid. Endings and beginnings. Neptune (modern) and Jupiter (traditional) are the rulers of Pisces. The polarity of the sign is Virgo. Pisces rules the feet, the lymphatic system, and the third eye. The stones corresponding to this sign are white diamond, aquamarine, and amethyst, and the metal is tin.

Pisces is the most spiritual and compassionate sign and their primary word is "**believe**." They are seen as highly sensitive, creative, and mystical beings. Pisces often struggle with boundaries and are extreme empaths, which can cause them to fall into the role of victim or martyr. Like the symbol of the fish swimming in two directions, it's the lesson of Pisces to live in the realms of the manifest and the mystical. If they can become comfortable with being an agent of spirit in the physical realm, they will avoid the escapist and addictive tendencies they may turn to on occasion. Pisces is associated with the energies of magic and the movies.

Fred Rogers (Mr. Rogers), Dr. Seuss, Ruth Bader Ginsburg, and Kurt Cobain were all born under the sign of Pisces.

CHAPTER FOUR

The Ascendant or Rising Sign and Decans

IN THIS CHAPTER, I will be discussing the 12 rising signs of the zodiac, also called the ascendants. Your rising sign is the sign that was on the eastern horizon at the moment of your birth and is the angle of nine o'clock on the astrological chart. More precisely, it's where the horizon line or plane intersects the ecliptic plane, the apparent plane of the Sun throughout the year from our perspective. Refer to Further Reading (see page 148) for resources on how to find your ascendant.

The ascendant is how people see you when they first meet you and what you present to others, often called the "persona" or "mask"—I prefer the term "receptionist," but any will work. It's the most visible aspect of a person when they show up in the world, the first impression others have of you. It also represents the conditioning brought by your birth and early childhood. All that you are is filtered through your ascendant. The exact time of birth is needed to accurately calculate your rising sign, as the ascendant is based on that date, time, and place.

Every chart has a ruling planet, and it's the planet that rules the sign on the ascendant that is the person's ruling planet. For example, if a chart has Sagittarius rising, the ruling planet is Jupiter. The ruling planet is one of the most important planets in any chart. The placement of that planet, and any planets that are conjunct or close to the ascendant, will modify the energy of the ascendant. Looking at all of this together is how we begin to create a picture of an individual, because although all people with the same rising sign will be similar, we are each unique once we begin to blend the whole chart.

We'll also be looking at the decans of each sign. Every sign spans 30°, and then each sign can be further broken down into 10° sections called decans. There are two systems of decans. I will be using the triplicity system, which assigns one of the same element of the sign to each decan. The first 10° belong to the sign itself, that is, Aries/Aries. The next 10° belong to the next sign in the same triplicity or element, that is, Aries/Leo, and the third 10° belong to the remaining sign in the triplicity, that is, Aries/Sagittarius. The other system of decans is the Chaldean system, which assigns one of the seven visible planets as ruler to each 10° decan. This system is less commonly used in modern astrology.

THE ASCENDANT

Let's look further into the ascendants for each sign of the zodiac. Any physical or characteristic descriptions are mostly based on observation by astrologers over time. Physical and other characteristics I describe throughout this book are based on generalities and should not be considered defining characteristics.

Aries Rising ♈

Aries rising is a day sign and these people are very active and straightforward.

Usually they are quick of movement and oriented toward sports and competitive activities—though their competitiveness is often self-directed. They often dive straight into things and go after what they want without always having thought things through. Aries rising does everything at full speed and likes to be on the move.

They are usually seen as pioneers and leaders, though they have difficulty finishing what they start. There will be no doubt when an Aries rising wants to be in relationship with you, whether as a friend or more. Their directness is a positive but can be overwhelming for some.

Mars is the ruling planet of those born with this ascendant and the placement of that ruling planet will give even more information about how this person operates in the world. Additionally, any planets close to the ascendant will temper the energy. For example, Saturn will really put the brakes on the fast energy of the rising sign.

Rihanna, John Lennon, and Samantha Fox were all born with Aries rising.

Taurus Rising ♉

I always think of Taurus rising as a strongly rooted tree with a big thick trunk, because they are steady and solid, immovable if others try to push them. In appearance, they often have a sturdy and solid look and usually like to be dressed in quality clothing, but nothing over the top. They have a very soothing presence, which makes them comfortable to be around unless you try to push them. They are, however, extremely loyal, to the point where they see others almost as belonging to them.

Taurus rising, a night sign, will usually move at a steady pace and doesn't like being pushed or rushed. Everything about them is sensual, in that they are attracted to nice smells, tastes, sounds, and touches. They may also have a pleasant voice.

Their ruling planet is Venus, and the placement of Venus will tell more about a specific individual. For example, if Venus is in Gemini, this may make an individual more flexible than the Taurus ascendant alone implies. Venus in Gemini may add to their sociability and the likelihood that they will use their pleasant voice in some way, such as for singing. Planets that conjunct the ascendant will also modify the energy.

Martin Luther King, Boy George, and Miley Cyrus were all born with Taurus rising.

Gemini Rising

Gemini-rising individuals are highly social but also the most chaotic of rising signs. The sign of the twins can argue from both sides of any subject, making them great debaters, but this makes them seem duplicitous, which can be difficult for some more sensitive signs.

Gemini rising are endlessly curious and witty and a joy to have around in a social environment. Their attention spans are short, however, so expect them to flit to the next thing very quickly. This restlessness gives them a nervous outer appearance at times, as they are constantly fidgeting. They are usually quite slender in appearance and will often have long artistic fingers, which you will usually see fiddling with something while they are talking. They are very good at multitasking, so although it may seem they are distracted and not listening, this isn't always the case.

Mercury is the ruling planet for Gemini and that planet's placement will say more about the person than the rising sign alone. A planet that conjuncts the ascendant will also temper this sign's energy. For example, Pluto conjuncting the Gemini ascendant will bring an intensity and depth not seen in all Gemini-rising people.

Bruce Springsteen, Ricky Martin, and Gene Wilder were all born with this rising sign.

Cancer Rising ♋

Individuals born with Cancer rising, a night sign, are highly sensitive and loving souls, the gentlest and most nurturing of people. Like the crab, which is the symbol of Cancer, they are shy and protective, preferring to slide sideways and quietly into any space. They also have a tendency toward moodiness and can either retreat into their shell or get needy when their mood is down. They are often described as "moon faced" and are often thought of as attractive. As Cancer rules the stomach, they may also have a tendency to gain weight and have digestive issues when feeling overwhelmed.

Their empathic "sponge-like" nature adds to this. Cancer rising feels everyone and everything around them and they are best served learning ways to protect their energy when they meet others, so they don't go into their moody hermit mode.

The Moon is the ruling planet of Cancer, and that represents mothering or nurturing energy, which explains why others are drawn to Cancer-rising people for care when it's needed. The placement of the Moon in the chart of the Cancer-rising person, however, provides a deeper level of understanding of the person. For example, the Moon in Aries will be more likely to want people to express their emotions directly and to also do this themselves.

Angelina Jolie, Julia Roberts, Tyra Banks, and John Travolta all have Cancer rising.

Leo Rising ♌

Leo-rising people are ruled by the Sun and it shows in their appearance, as they often have a lion's mane head of hair and a sunny round face. They are magnetic and light up any room when they enter, making an immediate impression. They are dramatic and demonstrative and love attention. They are sometimes loud, sometimes regal, but always commanding. They often dress for attention, as well.

Where this is less positive is if they don't get the attention and adulation they seek; their inner child can get bossy and have tantrums. Leo-rising people are big kids at heart and really just want to be loved and to survey their kingdom or queendom with benevolence. They make better leaders than workers, though they tend toward rashness at times.

The Sun is the center of our solar system and all the planets and the Earth revolve around it; this also suggests the character of the Leo-rising individual. They tend to think that the world revolves around them, and it often does. As the ruling planet, the placement of the Sun and any planets close to the ascendant modify the energy of the ascendant. A Virgo sun, for example, will be much less exuberant than some other placements.

"Persona" is a term used to describe the ascendant or rising sign. This was a term developed by Swiss psychiatrist Carl Jung, who characterized it as "a kind of mask, designed on the one hand to make a definite impression upon others, and on the other to conceal the true nature of the individual."

Jung, and most modern western astrologers, see the ascendant through this lens. We often identify more with our ascendant when young and begin the individuation process as we mature. It's entirely possible to overidentify with the social adaptation of the ascendant and for it to mask our authentic self through overadaptation to the outer image.

As the persona, in Jungian terms, is the public image, we often find public figures overidentifying with their public image.

To quote Jung, "One could say, with a little exaggeration, that the persona is that which in reality one is not, but which oneself, as well as others, think one is."

Astrology aims to encourage the person to individuate beyond the persona.

Muhammad Ali, Tina Turner, Meryl Streep, and George W. Bush were born with Leo rising.

Virgo Rising ♍

Virgo-rising people are the analysts and worriers of the zodiac. Their childhood may have had a parent obsessing over their health, weight, and appearance, which leaves them with a certain fastidiousness about these matters. Because they are standing back and analyzing situations and are quite shy, they can come across as reserved and standoffish, but they warm up as you get to know them. Once you do get to know them, you will find that their natural desire to help others makes them a loyal friend.

The tendency to overanalyze and seek perfection makes them anxiety-prone, especially if they aren't busy with projects and if they can't have everything in an order that suits them. They are usually neatly dressed and seem a little uptight.

As a mutable sign, they are not fixed in their ideas, but they have to review the evidence before they shift. "**Modest**" is a great word for Virgo-rising souls, and they usually have a graceful demeanor.

Mercury is the ruler of Virgo and the placement of Mercury and any planets close to the ascendant will modify the energy of the sign. For example, if Mercury is in the fixed sign Scorpio, their investigative quality will be much more piercing, as will their critical tendency.

Woody Allen, Hugh Hefner, Oscar Wilde, and Betty Ford were all born with Virgo rising.

Libra Rising ♎

Libra-rising individuals are very pleasant and charming to be around. They dislike conflict, so they are always seeking to mediate and play nice. They are generally attractive to look at and have a lovely round and sweet-looking appearance that adds to their charm. They are often slender. People are just attracted to Libra-rising individuals, who like to have relationships with others because they tend to see themselves through others' eyes and find it hard to be alone.

They can also have a tendency to have a passive-aggressive streak in relationships, as they may expect others to fulfill unrealistic expectations. This is a product of their well-known indecisiveness, as they are constantly trying to balance those Libra scales by looking at all sides.

The ruling planet of Libra rising is Venus in her less manifest energy of loving beauty, relationship, and harmony. The placement of Venus and any planets close to the ascendant will modify the rising sign. If Mars is conjuncting the ascendant, for example, the tendency toward passive aggression will be heightened.

Jennifer Aniston, Leonardo DiCaprio, Sally Field (her famous "you really like me" Oscar acceptance speech is classic Libra rising), and Venus Williams are all Libra rising.

Scorpio Rising ♏

Magnetic, intimidating, and intense are all words that describe those with Scorpio rising, a night sign. They are very private and even secretive about their inner life, which creates a mystique around them. They often have a slightly brooding appearance with penetrating eyes. Scorpio rising approaches everything with intensity, often to the point of obsession. They dig deeply into everything and have penetrative investigative traits, including seeming to see into others' souls.

Because of their very private nature, they often have problems expressing the deep swirl of emotions that their intense nature brings—sometimes even to themselves. They do, however, emanate a deep power and are usually passionate and creative about everything they do.

Pluto is the ruling planet of Scorpio-rising people and the placement of Pluto will modify the rising sign. For example,

The Descendant

The polarity point to the ascendant or rising sign is the descendant, or seventh-house cusp, which is the sign that was on the western horizon from the perspective of the date, time, and place of birth.

The descendant is an important consideration when exploring what kind of person you are attracted to and whom you attract in all significant relationships. This can also indicate blind spots within you that you aspire to personally develop through partnerships. It could be said that your ascendant is day energy, or what you put out into the world, and your descendant is night energy, or what you receive from others through partnership.

The blind spots the descendant represents are called the "disowned self." In other words, we see something in others that irritates us until we recognize that it's actually a part of us that needs acknowledgement. For example, you may find it irritating that your partner is detached emotionally if you have Aquarius on the descendant, but once you become aware of it, you are able to realize that it's actually something you need to work on within yourself—it can be a big awakening. In other words, what felt like aloofness can become a sense of freedom. This is also known as mirror work, where we transmute any irritating qualities into positive traits to be developed. This is an important factor to consider when looking at compatibility.

someone with Pluto in the third house will be more likely to be chatty and less focused. Planets that conjunct the ascendant also modify the impact of the rising sign.

Aretha Franklin, David Lynch, Robin Williams, and Prince were all born with Scorpio rising.

Sagittarius Rising ♐

Sagittarius-rising people are fun and freedom loving. They have an air of enthusiasm and optimism about life that few other rising signs have. They are adventurers and are always seeking experiences that will enhance their lives, sometimes traveling extensively and living in places other than where they were born. They also travel in their minds and often have a big library of books or many books next to their bed.

Those born under this rising sign are often so full of excitement and opinions gained from their explorations that they tend to lack tact and may suffer from foot-in-mouth syndrome. Their likeability and sense of humor generally stop them from getting into too much trouble, however. They are also seen as a little naive.

In appearance, they are often quite tall and rangy and are on the move much of the time, as if they are in a hurry to get to the next experience—which they probably are.

Sagittarius rising's ruling planet is Jupiter and the placement of that or planets near the ascendant will modify the sign. Saturn on the ascendant, for example, will make this person less outgoing and more inclined to appear serious.

Jamie Lee Curtis, Arsenio Hall, Princess Diana, and Hans Christian Andersen were all born with Sagittarius rising.

Capricorn Rising ♑

Capricorn-rising people are the most ambitious of the zodiac and are very serious and work-oriented. They are definitely not the party animals of the zodiac. They do often have a dry sense of humor with impeccable timing, however. Their appearance is usually lean and quite angular with bright eyes and they are often dressed for success, preferring an earthy palette of clothing colors.

Because of their serious demeanor, Capricorn-rising people can come across

as quite cold emotionally, though they really aren't—they just don't show emotion easily. Capricorn-rising individuals may have had a difficult childhood or been given a lot of responsibility early in life. They usually loosen up with age. These individuals tend to like security and to be the provider for their family and partners, but there's also an undercurrent of fear of not being or doing enough.

Saturn is the ruling planet for Capricorn and both Saturn's placement and any other planets near the ascendant will modify the rising sign energy. For example, if Saturn is in Pisces, they will be more intuitive and connected to their creative side.

Queen Elizabeth II, Jane Fonda, Taylor Swift, and Joseph Stalin were all born with Capricorn rising.

Aquarius Rising ♒

Those born with Aquarius rising, a day sign, are quirky, curious, and more than a little rebellious. They are friendly and love a good intellectual meeting of the minds, especially if it involves the subject of how to save the world, or at least a part of the world. They also love a good debate and play devil's advocate well. They are humanitarians, often idealistic and future-oriented, and can paint their vision of what a more egalitarian world would look like from a progressive viewpoint, as they often truly want a real "humanhood" for people of all persuasions. They seem quite emotionally detached while also caring about the world as activists.

Aquarius rising usually has a youthful appearance with a medium stature and they tend to be drawn to wearing clothes seen as quirky or individualistic in some way.

Uranus is the ruling planet of Aquarius and the placement of that planet will modify the rising sign, as will any planets close to the ascendant. For example, if the Moon is close to the ascendant, they may be a little warmer and more emotionally engaged.

Barack Obama, David Bowie, Nicki Minaj, and Carl Jung were all born with Aquarius rising.

Pisces Rising ♓

Pisces-rising people are the dreamers of the zodiac, as they seem to float in the realms of fantasy, and they are very soft hearted and compassionate. As a mutable water sign, they are very reflective of those around them and are empathic sponges, often having a shape-shifting quality that mirrors those around them. They are imaginative and creative and one of the least grounded rising signs, so they operate best with relationships that steady

them—they are susceptible to manipulative people.

Because of their extreme sensitivity, they are often vulnerable to drugs of all kinds, including prescribed drugs. They may also be prone to depression because the world doesn't live up to their dreams and ideals. They are often beautiful and have a shimmery, ethereal appearance that is charming to most people. Kind people want to protect them.

Pisces rising's ruling planet is Neptune and the placement of Neptune will modify how the rising sign works. For example, Neptune in Taurus will mean the person is more grounded and connected to earthly things. Planets near the ascendant will also modify how the rising sign works.

Michael Jackson, Whitney Houston, Robert Redford (setting up Sundance, a leading independent film festival, is a classic example), and Bruno Mars all have Pisces rising.

DECANS

A decan is a subdivision of 10° of an astrological sign. Decans are complex and have been developed from Egyptian times, when they were first based on 36 fixed stars, dividing 360° into 36 sections. These decans were merged with the 12 signs of the zodiac in the first century CE, when the Egyptian and Mesopotamian traditions converged.

From that point, two systems emerged, and we are going to explore the triplicity system to give more information about each person. Each person will have their sun in a decan, which deepens the understanding of that placement. The dates in each decan refer to your birth date.

The Decans of Aries

The first decan, ruled by Mars, is the Aries decan. People born under this decan are the true pioneers of the zodiac and are very action-oriented, driven, and courageous. They approach life with the zeal of a child and have a lovely innocence in their enthusiasm. You are in this decan if your sun is from 0° to 9° Aries, and approximate dates for this decan are March 21 through March 31.

The second decan of Aries is ruled by the Sun and is the Leo decan. The Sun and Leo bring a regal quality to these people, who like to shine in the world and receive a lot of attention. The fixed quality of Leo brings a certain immovable quality to the leadership energy of this decan, meaning that they stick to their aims no matter what others want. This can be the energy of the pompous leader. You are in this decan if your sun is from 10° to 19° Aries, and approximate

dates for this decan are April 1 through April 11.

The third decan of Aries is ruled by Jupiter and is the Sagittarius decan. Jupiter brings an expansiveness and seeking quality to the sign of Aries. Aries energy is usually focused, but this decan likes to explore and search for their personal truth. They are very much individuals who go their own way. You are in this decan if your sun is from 20° to 29° Aries, and approximate dates for this decan are April 12 through April 21.

The Decans of Taurus

The first decan, ruled by Venus, is the Taurus decan. This person is stable and very connected to the Earth and the material world. This decan has a very instinctive body knowledge, which means that they love to nourish their body with good food, things that are tactile, and things that generally make them feel good. Overindulgence and inflexibility can be the downside of this energy, but they do have a very peaceful and loving presence and are usually very sensual and sexual. You are in this decan if your sun is from 0° to 9° Taurus, and approximate dates for this decan are April 22 to May 1.

The second decan is ruled by Mercury and is the Virgo decan. The influence of Mercury and Virgo brings more flexibility to the usually stubborn Taurus energy. These people are pragmatic and realistic but in a very quiet and unassuming way. The sensitivity of Virgo and Mercury can make them come across as dull to others of a more visionary and idealistic nature, as they are the people who will always tell others they aren't living in reality. You are in this decan if your sun is from 10° to 19° Taurus, and approximate dates for this decan are May 2 to May 11.

The third decan of Taurus is ruled by Saturn and is the Capricorn decan. These people are a little more blocked off from the indulgent energy of Taurus, as they can be too busy building and climbing to enjoy the fruits of their labor—though they do still love to own the good things in life. They have a more austere presence and may seem boring to some. They are, however, master builders of solid and lasting structures in their life, whether it be a career, a home base, or a family. Once you get to know the person behind the urge to build, they can be quite funny and sensual under the surface. You are in this decan if your sun is from 20° to 29° Taurus, and approximate dates for this decan are May 12 to May 21.

The Decans of Gemini

The first decan of Gemini is ruled by Mercury and is the Gemini decan. Those born with the sun in this decan are extremely curious, and you will always find them taking in information from a variety of sources. They are also likely to be scattered and easily distracted as they flit from one thing to another. This is also known as shiny object, or squirrel, syndrome. Their mind is very quick, and they make sense of a lot of information in a detached way, but because of their tendency to be easily distracted, they rarely go deeply into any one subject. You are in this decan if your sun is from 0° to 9° Gemini, and approximate dates for this decan are May 22 to June 1.

The second decan of Gemini is ruled by Venus and is the Libra decan. These are social people who want to be around and converse with others as much as possible. They are, like all Geminis, curious and want to know all about you and what makes you tick. Their natural curiosity also draws them to study art or the wonders of nature, for example. They have a tendency to see themselves through the eyes of others, however, and that can lead to difficulty making any decisions without others' input. They make really good mediators, as they see the good in people and can present that to the other side in a negotiation. You are in this decan if your sun is from 10° to 19° Gemini, and approximate dates for this decan are June 2 to June 11.

The third decan of Gemini is ruled by Uranus and is the Aquarius decan. These are the big-picture thinkers who are able to come up with innovative concepts. They are the most emotionally detached and can, for that reason, seem distant from others. However, that's because they are taking the bird's-eye view and seeing the connections needed to help humanity as a whole. Their breadth of knowledge is enormous and their vision is like a giant puzzle put together with seemingly disparate pieces. They are usually very friendly but will want to talk about some big ideas rather than engage in small talk. You are in this decan if your sun is from 20° to 29° Gemini, and approximate dates for this decan are June 12 to June 21.

The Decans of Cancer

The first decan of Cancer is ruled by the Moon and is the Cancer decan. This makes for an extremely emotionally sensitive and compassionate person who nurtures and cares for those they love with unending capacity for an emotional connection. This can, however, lead to identifying with this role to such a degree that they never communicate their own emotional needs. This can lead to insecurity and emotionally manipulative behavior. They are also likely to find it difficult to let go of past hurt feelings. They love with intensity, which can be comforting for some and overwhelming for others. You are in this decan if your

sun is from 0° to 9° Cancer, and approximate dates for this decan are June 22 to July 1.

The second decan of Cancer is ruled by Pluto and is the Scorpio decan. These people's emotions are as deep as the deepest ocean and, like the ocean at those depths, those emotions can be hard to access and express. Because of this, these people can seem almost emotionless and their natural reserve adds to this. Of course, this is only the surface impression because the opposite is true. They feel so very deeply that they are willing to do anything for those they love, to the point of self-sacrifice. The depth of Scorpio can also make them possessive of those they love, but they make amazing listeners and can hold space for others like no one else. You are in this decan if your sun is from 10° to 19° Cancer, and approximate dates for this decan are July 2 to July 11.

The third decan of Cancer is ruled by Neptune and is the Pisces decan. These are the most sensitive and gentle people you will ever meet. They have a very ethereal presence, as their moods shift in response to all that is around them. It's often hard to know what they are really feeling, and they themselves are not always aware. They, like those of the first decan, are tireless when caring for those they love, but there's the addition of a tendency to feel like a victim when they feel others take advantage of them. These people must learn to create better personal boundaries. You are in this decan if your sun is from 20° to 29° Cancer, and approximate dates for this decan are July 12 to July 21.

The Decans of Leo

The first decan of Leo is ruled by the Sun and is the Leo decan. This is the ruler of all, or at least that is how this person sees themselves. They see themselves as special and entitled to be leaders or adored in all that they do, in the nicest possible way. They feel as if they were born to be first and, in many respects, they are right, as they radiate warmth and a regal presence. Leo is ruled by the heart and many belonging to this decan are benevolent leaders, but they often lack humility. When others don't quite see them as they see themselves or treat them with the attention they feel they deserve, they can feel very hurt. You are in this decan if your sun is from 0° to 9° Leo, and approximate dates for this decan are July 22 to August 1.

The second decan of Leo is ruled by Jupiter and is the Sagittarius decan. These are the gamblers and risk takers of the sign, as the influence of Jupiter brings an expansive vibe and a sense of being so lucky that all they touch will turn to gold. It often does. They also tend to shower that sense of well-being onto those around them because they are generous to a fault. This tendency toward risk-taking can also lead them to over-extend at times, but they usually fall on their feet. You are in this decan if your sun is from 10° to 19° Leo, and approximate dates for this decan are August 2 to August 11.

The third decan of Leo is ruled by Mars and is the Aries decan. This is the warrior lion who will go out into the world with a sense of righteousness and possibility, who truly believes they can achieve anything they desire. Their will is so strong and desire so great that they often do achieve what they set their heart on. The fixed quality of Leo makes them stick to achieving those desires but can also make them stubborn and resistant to any input from others, and they will rarely admit to making mistakes. They are very open and honest, however, no matter what others say or think. You are in this decan if your sun is from 20° to 29° Leo, and approximate dates for this decan are August 12 through August 21.

The Decans of Virgo

The first decan of Virgo is ruled by Mercury and is the Virgo decan. Those born under this decan have a very intellectual and extremely rational mind. They are productive to a fault and always seek to make their day function more productively so that they can be more useful with their time. They enjoy intellectual relationships in which they can discuss plans and ideas with those around them. They are also great worriers and their inner self-critic is probably the strongest of all people in the zodiac, as they are constantly analyzing everything. The mutable energy of the decan means they are often course-correcting, which can be both a blessing and a curse. You are in this decan if your sun is from 0° to 9° Virgo, and approximate dates for this decan are August 22 to September 1.

The second decan of Virgo is ruled by Saturn and is the Capricorn decan. The initiating energy of Saturn and Capricorn relieves some of the potential analysis paralysis of Virgo and encourages them to take action to create structures that give them material security. They tend to be overachievers, seeking to keep building and making money, and are investors more than spenders because that gives them the sense of achievement they need. They can also throw in the towel on some projects if they feel they are failing. They are very responsible and great managers but their drive to achieve can mean they miss out on the lighter and more fun side of life. You are in this decan if your sun is from 10° to 19° Virgo, and approximate

dates for this decan are September 2 to September 11.

The third decan of Virgo is ruled by Venus and is the Taurus decan. The soothing presence of Venus and the steadying influence of Taurus make this decan of Virgo less highly strung than others. Virgo likes to make things with their hands, and you might find this decan being creative in any field that requires them to mold or use other earthy materials, such as sculpture or finger painting. These are slower moving people and generally quite reserved and self-contained. They also like to dress well and look good, but in a very neat manner. They are rarely flamboyant. You are in this decan if your sun is from 20° to 29° Virgo, and approximate dates for this decan are September 12 to September 21.

The Decans of Libra

The first decan of Libra is ruled by Venus and is the Libra decan. These people are lovers of beauty, pleasure, and others. They love harmony, peace, and for life to be smooth and lovely. They are happiest when in relationships, and yet the shadow of Libra is that they can become argumentative at times and will sometimes argue just for the sake of it. They also have a keen sense of what works in business, and a balanced first decan will utilize that and create a healthy work-life balance. When they are as balanced as they can be, they tend to live in a place that is peaceful and beautiful, both outwardly and inwardly. You are in this decan if your sun is from 0° to 9° Libra, and approximate dates for this decan are September 22 to October 1.

The second decan of Libra is ruled by Uranus and is the Aquarius decan. These people are more individualistic than the other decans of Libra, and they are more drawn to the intellect of others in their lives rather than how things look visually. They are also drawn to needing more personal space to find the balance that Libra needs. You are in this decan if your sun is from 10° to 19° Libra, and approximate dates for this decan are October 2 to October 11.

The third decan of Libra is ruled by Mercury and is the Gemini decan. These are charming people who can woo others with their words, but they are also more changeable and restless, which can upset the needed balance and harmony integral to Libra. They are highly sociable and need to converse with others on a regular basis. You are in this decan if your sun is from 20° to 29° Libra, and approximate dates for this decan are October 12 to October 21.

The Decans of Scorpio

The first decan of Scorpio is ruled by Pluto and is the Scorpio decan. These people are deep and extremely intense. They may, almost unconsciously, play power games with others as they try to fulfill their deep longings and desires. They are often possessive and can be obsessive, as they desire to merge with those with whom they are in a relationship. They are not the easiest people to be around, but they love very deeply if you can stand the heat. You are in this decan if your sun is from 0° to 9° Scorpio, and approximate dates for this decan are October 22 to November 1.

The second decan of Scorpio is ruled by Neptune and is the Pisces decan. Those born under this decan are very intuitive and seductive. They magnetize others with a glamour that sometimes doesn't reveal what's really going on. Their imaginations are quite magical, and their ideals are high but at times totally unrealistic. You are in this decan if your sun is from 10° to 19° Scorpio, and approximate dates for this decan are November 2 to November 11.

The third decan of Scorpio is ruled by the Moon and is the Cancer decan. The nurturing and loving qualities of the Moon and Cancer soften the intensity of Scorpio considerably, though their receptive nature still wants to connect with others at a deep emotional level. These people have great loyalty but with a higher level of trust. You are in this decan if your sun is from 20° to 29°

Scorpio, and approximate dates for this decan are November 12 to November 21.

The Decans of Sagittarius

The first decan of Sagittarius is the Sagittarius decan, ruled by Jupiter. These people are adventurous and optimistic, though they may lack tact at times. They often study higher philosophies and principles, including those of various religions, and tend to be lifelong learners. They also can tend to be on the dogmatic side and preach what they know. You are in this decan if your sun is from 0° to 9° Sagittarius, and approximate dates for this decan are November 22 to December 1.

The second decan of Sagittarius is ruled by Mars and is the Aries decan. These people may be accident-prone, as Sagittarius in general tends to gallop everywhere—combined with the head-first energy of Mars, they may not always look where they are going. They are constantly challenging themselves and are usually completely open and honest. These people need action and movement. You are in this decan if your sun is from 10° to 19° Sagittarius, and approximate dates for this decan are December 2 to December 11.

The third decan of Sagittarius is the Leo decan, which is ruled by the Sun. This is another risk-taking placement, and the combination can lead them to

gamble in life as they seek adventure and experience. They are people of integrity but also can let their pride get in the way as they aim high, and that can lead to falls. You are in this decan if your sun is from 20° to 29° Sagittarius, and approximate dates for this decan are December 12 to December 21.

The Decans of Capricorn

The first decan of Capricorn is ruled by Saturn and is the Capricorn decan. These people have great determination and can move mountains. They are very serious and responsible. Because they have double the responsible energy of Capricorn, they also can have double the fear of not being enough and must be wary of working too hard because of their fear of failure. You are in this decan if your sun is from 0° to 9° Capricorn, and approximate dates for this decan are December 22 to January 1.

The second decan of Capricorn is ruled by Venus and is the Taurus decan. The middle decans are often the most balanced and the middle Capricorn decan is no different. The energy of Venus and Taurus means that these people are still responsible and determined but will also make sure they relax and enjoy the comforts their achievements bring. They are happier with a slower approach to achievement. You are in this decan if your sun is from 10° to

19° Capricorn, and approximate dates for this decan are January 2 to January 11.

The third decan of Capricorn is ruled by Mercury and is the Virgo decan. These people are more impatient than the first two decans of this sign and are always seeking to make everything they do more functional, so that they can get to the next thing faster. They have more of a nervy quality, as they can feel held back by the relentless determination of Capricorn. You are in this decan if your sun is from 20° to 29° Capricorn, and approximate dates for this decan are January 12 to January 21.

The Decans of Aquarius

The first decan of Aquarius is the Aquarius decan, ruled by Uranus, and these people are real individualists and nonconformists. They are progressive-minded, sociable humanitarians, though they often have only a small circle of friends. They are always thinking up new plans and ideas and their minds are rarely still; their overthinking can lead to anxiety if they don't get some solitary downtime. You are in this decan if your sun is from 0° to 9° Aquarius, and approximate dates for this decan are January 22 through February 1.

The second decan of Aquarius is ruled by Mercury and is the Gemini decan. These people have a similar nature to the first decan but with a lighter feel. They are still individuals but are more social and curious about the world rather than only abstract ideas. They are often literature lovers. They are also usually great communicators with a desire to teach all that they study to others. You are in this decan if your sun is from 10° to 19° Aquarius, and approximate dates for this decan are February 2 through February 11.

The third decan of Aquarius is the Libra decan, ruled by Venus. These people are usually great politicians by nature because they are very good with people and really care about bettering the lives of others. They can usually see the best in people and want to help bring that out. They are often very graceful and willowy. You are in this decan if your sun is from 20° to 29° Aquarius, and approximate dates for this decan are February 12 through February 21.

The Decans of Pisces

The first decan of Pisces is ruled by Neptune and is the Pisces decan. These people are almost pure psychic sponges, sensitive to all that is around them. They are highly intuitive and connected to the collective unconscious. They are usually attracted to mystical experiences, since they already inhabit those realms. They are easily taken advantage of, as they have few boundaries and they often seem to be a walking nebulous cloud of dreams and creativity. You are in this decan if your sun is from 0° to 9° Pisces, and approximate dates for this decan are February 22 through March 1.

The second decan of Pisces is the Cancer decan, ruled by the Moon. These people are creative romantics but also crave security and safety the most of all the decans. They are loyal to a fault to those they love and can be very needy if they don't feel secure. Their artistic and homemaking abilities will blossom when they are secure. Those born under this decan need the security of the home and close family bonds, but they also need a lot of alone time within that structure.

You are in this decan if your Sun is from 10° to 19° Pisces, and approximate dates for this decan are March 2 through March 11.

The third decan of Pisces is ruled by Pluto and is the Scorpio decan. Those born under this decan are often drawn to the realms of the hidden and the taboo, such as the realms of magic, mediumship, and death. They are often finely connected to the other side and may even see spirits. At the very least, they are deeply intuitive and can sense what's happening within those around them. You are in this decan if your sun is from 20° to 29° Pisces, and approximate dates for this decan are March 12 through March 21.

CHAPTER FIVE

Planets and Other Essential Bodies

THE ASTROLOGICAL CHART is created using many elements. This chapter looks at the planets and other essential bodies, which can be described as the "what" in the chart, with the signs being "how" the planets work in you, and the houses being the "where," or areas of life.

The "what" in your chart represents such things as your emotions, your drive, your love nature, your mind, or to word it differently, integral parts of the self. The different signs show how those parts of the self are represented in a person and whether that is, for example, in a more enthusiastic manner or a more reserved manner. The house, or the "where," indicates the areas of life in which the planet and sign operate most prevalently in individuals.

Historically, astrology used the two luminaries, Sun and Moon, and the five visible planets: Mercury, Venus, Mars, Jupiter, and Saturn. Modern astrology, however, also uses more recently discovered cosmic bodies. Some of these are included here, and others will be discussed later in the book.

In part 2 (see page 75), you will learn how to structure and interpret a birth chart. These sections will be used as a reference as you integrate all of the parts of the chart to create a holistic picture of the self.

THE SUN ☉

The Sun is the central organizing principle of both the solar system and the self. It's the core identity and the Sun in your chart energizes you. The Sun is day energy, as the Sun clearly shines in the day and is an inhalation of breath that energizes our bodies. Like the Sun in the solar system, everything else revolves around this shining core. The Sun rules the sign of Leo and the heart, and this indicates that the Sun is the heart of you. The Sun is seen as a masculine or yang energy in modern western culture, but in many other traditions the Sun has been seen as feminine because of its life-giving qualities.

The Sun functions as your CEO or conductor, and when you are tuned into the energy of your personal sun sign then you are operating at your most aligned. The Sun also represents self-expression, sense of purpose, creativity, and the ego in the healthiest of senses.

The highest expression of Sun energy is the benevolent leader who lights up the lives of others and is energized by how they shine light on others. In its lesser expression, the Sun can be boastful and egotistical. Like the actual Sun in the solar system, however, the energy of the sun within us can be dulled or blocked by other placements, and a sun sign that is blocked makes it more difficult to express that energy.

THE MOON ☽

The Moon represents your emotional needs and your relationship to feelings. It is night energy and the energy of an exhalation as we relax at the end of the day. The sign of Cancer and the fourth house are both ruled by the Moon. The Moon also represents your relationship to family, home, and your ancestors.

The Moon is receptive and reflective, giving out no light of its own. Because of that, western cultures have designated the Moon as yin or feminine energy because of the portrayal of the feminine as passive. There are other traditions, however, that believe the Sun is the ovum and the Moon the sperm. The Moon is visibly night energy, where we exhale, rest, and recover our energy.

The Moon is our basis of security and often represents the mother, or the person who "mothered" you in your early life. The Moon rules body rhythms, including menstrual cycles and the cycles of sleep, and it is a commonly held belief that we sleep less and have more energy when the Moon is full, and we are more inwardly focused and need alone time in the dark of the Moon. As our Moon placement says a lot about our response to the outer world, the actual phases of the Moon affect us also. There's an ebb and flow to all lunar energy.

MERCURY ☿

Mercury is both day and night energy and an inhale and exhale, since Mercury rules the signs of Gemini, the twins, and

Virgo, service and usefulness. Mercury is the most nonbinary of the planetary bodies, and the fact that the planet rules both the yang (day) air sign of Gemini and the yin (earth) night sign of Virgo indicates this. Mercury is the first of the personal planets after the luminaries, the Sun and Moon.

Mercury represents the mind, communication, the messenger, detail, technical ability, perception, and learning. Mercury is also coordination, how our mind tells our neural pathways to coordinate.

Depending on the placement of Mercury and how we are embodying our Mercury, it can be curious, witty, sociable, and versatile or nervy, overconcerned with detail, and even highly strung. Mercury is also associated with the trickster archetype—the fact that the planet appears to go retrograde three to four times each year is indicative of its trickster nature, because Mercury retrograde is renowned for technical snafus and miscommunications. The trickster archetype is one that turns conventional rules and behavior on their heads.

Mercury is associated with Hermes, the messenger of the gods. It is the closest planet to the Sun, our core, and transmits information from the core to Earth. Mercury travels closely with the Sun from our perspective and is always in the same sign as the Sun or one of the two adjacent signs.

VENUS ♀

Venus is generally known as the planet of love and, of course, modern astrology has defined that as feminine, despite the fact that Venus rules both Libra, a day air sign, and Taurus, a night earth sign. Like Mercury, Venus is both day and night and an exhale and inhale. Modern astrology's definitions reflect gender bias and why some have never identified with such concepts as "men are from Mars and women are from Venus."

Venus is the second of the personal planets, the second planet from the Sun and the closest to the Earth. Venus, like Mercury, travels closely with the Sun from our perspective and is always either in the same sign as or in one of the adjacent signs to the Sun.

Venus rules the senses and, therefore, symbolizes the relationship to all that can be seen, touched, heard, smelled, and tasted, which includes people, nature, money, food, and things. Venus also symbolizes values, the arts, beauty, sensuality, harmony, and mediation—as well as indecisiveness, inertia, and overindulgence.

Venus has a cycle that reflects a more complex and binary energy: When it rises above the Sun, Venus is the "morning star," known as Phosphorus or Lucifer, the light bearer, an outgoing yang (day) Venus. When it moves to set after the Sun, Venus is the evening star, or Hesperus, which is a much more receptive yin (night) placement. It's good practice to look at this, as well as sign and house placement and aspects to other planets, to give you a full picture of an individual's Venus.

MARS ♂

Mars is the last of the personal planets and the only personal planet to be farther from the Sun than the Earth. As Mars leads us to the outer reaches of the solar system and away from the Sun, the energy of the planet itself is more outgoing. Mars rules Aries, the pioneer of the zodiac. Interestingly, Mars also rules Scorpio in traditional astrology.

Traditional astrology generally refers to practices that use only the planets and essential bodies that were visible to the naked eye, so that they assigned rulership of signs to planetary bodies from the moon through Saturn. As traditional ruler of Scorpio, the red planet displays a night, exhale designation. In modern astrology, Mars is yang (day) energy.

Mars symbolizes action, drive, courage, leadership, assertion, aggression, and anger. Mars is often said to symbolize fighting and competition, but it must be pointed out that Venus-ruled Libra rules war itself, as well as peace. Again, astrology is more complex than some might think.

Mars is associated with physicality and competition in general. Knives and guns are also images that connect to Mars. Mars is passion, impatience, and life force, and as such is an inhalation of breath. Without Mars, we would get little done in life. Mars helps us fulfill our desires. Mars is our animalistic nature and we all have that to a greater or lesser degree, dependent on the placement in the individual horoscope. In its night incarnation as the traditional ruler of Scorpio, Mars is penetrative and passionate.

JUPITER ♃

Jupiter is often called the first of the social planets, as we move farther away from the Sun, and represents a transition from the personal planets to the outer, more recently discovered, transpersonal or collective planets. Jupiter is a day/inhale planet as ruler of fire sign Sagittarius. As traditional ruler of Pisces, Jupiter is night or exhale. This diffuse energy must be taken into account as you look at the planet in an individual's chart.

Jupiter rules Sagittarius, the sign of truth seeking and belief, and the ninth house. Jupiter is the guru or teacher of the zodiac and symbolizes the god energy. In the Roman pantheon there was originally a council of six gods and six goddesses called *Dei Consentes*, but Jupiter became the primary god later in Roman culture.

The planet Jupiter, as god of the sky, symbolizes freedom, optimism, generosity, luck, expansion, breadth, and truth. Jupiter is the prophet, the sage, the world traveler and explorer. Jupiter also symbolizes grandiosity, inflation, the braggart, and the soap box.

Jupiter is often seen as the lucky planet, and this can be true, but Jupiter also represents overexpansion and overdoing of all kinds.

SATURN ♄

Saturn is the second of the social planets and the last of the original planets visible to the eye that were used in traditional astrology. Saturn rules the yin earth sign Capricorn, and yet characteristics that are traditionally seen as masculine are attributed to the planet. We must remember that all genders have these qualities within them. Saturn is a night, colder energy and is an exhalation of breath as ruler of Capricorn. However, as traditional ruler of Uranus, Saturn also exhibits day or inhale energy. Please take into account the day or night energy of the sign placement of Saturn when you interpret your chart. Saturn is also associated with the 10th house.

Saturn symbolizes external authority, as is fitting for what was thought of as the outer limit of our solar system. Other symbols for Saturn are the parent or father—or the energy of the parent who exhibited more yang energy. Saturn symbolizes boundaries, rules and limitations, fear, denial, and control. Saturn also symbolizes maturity, tradition, sensory reality, and elderhood.

Saturn has been much maligned for these qualities at times, but boundaries and a sensible awareness of limitations are important to be able to build the structures of your life. It's where we close the door, literally or figuratively, to recoup after the action-oriented energy of the day. Saturn can be the backbone and anchor of your life if you choose to work with the placement in your chart.

URANUS ♅

Uranus is the first of the more recently discovered transpersonal planets, those that are not visible to the naked eye. Uranus was discovered by William Herschel in 1781 and it was quite a shock to discover a planet beyond the boundary of the previously known solar system. Uranus rules Aquarius and the 11th house. The discovery of Uranus opened up the discovery of collective, larger forces, which led to opening the minds of astrologers. Concepts such as the soul and major planetary cycles had previously been limited by what was thought to be a closed system with Saturn at the outer limit. This indicates the awakening energy and shattered boundaries that Uranus symbolizes. Uranus also has a spin axis that is 98° to the perpendicular, which sets it apart from other cosmic bodies.

Uranus represents individuality, uniqueness, unconventionality, and independence. Uranus is the revolutionary and the rebel. As such, this is a day energy of action and activity and an inhale. Where Uranus sits in a horoscope shows where you will be called to go your own way and break free from the status quo. Uranus is the inventive genius who is open to information and ideas that have not been thought of before, or where connections have not been made before.

NEPTUNE ♆

Neptune, the second of the transpersonal planets, was discovered in 1846. Like the nebulous nature of Neptune itself, it was discovered by mathematical prediction—based on hypotheses that a planetary body was disturbing the orbit of Uranus—rather than simply through empirical observation. We now know that Galileo actually observed Neptune in the 17th century, possibly mistaking it for a star. These confusing discovery experiences are emblematic of Neptune's symbolism.

Neptune rules Pisces and the 12th house and symbolizes illusion, confusion, consciousness itself, psychic sensitivity, and trance-like creative energy. All realms of mysticism and mystery are symbolized by Neptune, as are addiction and victimization complexes.

Dwarf Planets

The discovery of what are currently called dwarf planets by astronomers is changing astrology further and at a faster rate than ever before; these discoveries coincide with the shift of ages from the Age of Pisces to the Age of Aquarius.

Astrological ages each represent a major time period in history. Each astrological age lasts approximately 2,160 years and we move through all the ages over 25,920 years. The Age of Pisces began around the same time as the birth of Christianity, and we are currently in the transition between the Age of Pisces and the next age, the Age of Aquarius. (Ages go backward through the signs.)

The discovery of Eris in 2005 shook the world of astronomy and led to the new designation of "dwarf planet" in 2006, as well as the demotion of Pluto and promotion of Ceres, formerly believed to be an asteroid, to the new designation.

Since the discovery of Eris, several other dwarf planets have been discovered, including Haumea and MakeMake, with Sedna, Orcus, Quaoar, Varuna, Ixion, and a few other trans-Neptunian objects in the Kuiper belt being considered. Some estimates suggest that there are at least 100 objects that may be classified as dwarf planets that have yet to be discovered in the exploration of the Kuiper belt—and thousands more beyond.

Many astrologers are beginning to explore some of these objects in their work, but because this is a newly discovered realm of study with new discoveries happening all the time, this book will only cover Pluto and Ceres.

Neptune is boundaryless and sacrificial, but also healing and gentle. Neptune energy dissolves and makes all that it touches more nebulous. As a receptive and feeling planet, Neptune is night energy or an exhale.

PLUTO ♇

Pluto is the last of the transpersonal planets used in most modern astrology. In fact, Pluto is no longer a planet according to the astronomical world, as it got demoted after the discovery of dwarf planet Eris. Asteroid Ceres got promoted to dwarf-planet status at the same time, creating a whole new classification of cosmic bodies. This did not, however, diminish the power inherent in Pluto. Since Pluto is the energy of transformation, is it any surprise that it, alongside the newly discovered dwarf planets, is transforming astrology further? Pluto rules Scorpio and the eighth house and is a night, or exhale, energy.

Pluto symbolizes personal transformation, psychological depth, and the soul's desire to evolve. As the guardian of the underworld, Pluto guards our personal resources that are buried in the depths of our psyche. All things that are seen by many as taboo are symbolized by Pluto, including sexuality, repression, depression, and obsessive behaviors. Underlying reality and the realms of karmic wounds are symbolized by Pluto. It's an intense and powerful energy, which represents both personal empowerment and powerlessness.

PLANETARY DIGNITIES AND DEBILITIES

All planets are not only considered to have rulership over or domicile in one or more signs, they are also considered to be more aligned with certain signs and less so with others. These are called dignities and debilities. Consideration of dignities and debilities after rulership will deepen your understanding of the planets and signs in a horoscope.

The four essential dignities are:

- **Rulership:** This is where the planet is most at home (reference your individual sign in this book, where I note rulership).
- **Detriment:** When the planet is in the opposite sign to its rulership, it is said to be weakened.
- **Exaltation:** This is the sign that provides the best expression of the planet after its domicile.
- **Fall:** When the planet is in the opposite sign to its exaltation, it's said to be at its weakest.

If a planet falls in none of these, it is said to be peregrine and aspects become more crucial. It must be noted that experience shows that detriment and fall don't always play out negatively, especially when well-aspected.

This is a brief list of planetary dignities and debilities:

The Sun: Rulership in Leo, detriment in Aquarius, exaltation in Aries, fall in Libra

The Moon: Rulership in Cancer, detriment in Capricorn, exaltation in Taurus, fall in Scorpio

Mercury: Rulership in Gemini and Virgo, detriment in Sagittarius and Pisces, exaltation in Virgo, fall in Pisces

Venus: Rulership in Taurus and Libra, detriment in Scorpio and Aries, exaltation in Pisces, fall in Virgo

Mars: Rulership in Aries and Scorpio, detriment in Libra and Taurus, exaltation in Capricorn, fall in Cancer

Jupiter: Rulership in Sagittarius and Pisces, detriment in Gemini and Virgo, exaltation in Cancer, fall in Capricorn

Saturn: Rulership in Capricorn and Aquarius, detriment in Cancer and Leo, exaltation in Libra, fall in Aries

Uranus: Rulership in Aquarius, detriment in Leo, exaltation in Scorpio, fall in Taurus

Neptune: Rulership in Pisces, detriment in Virgo, exaltation in Leo (or Cancer, depending on whose work you read), fall in Aquarius (or Capricorn)

Pluto: Rulership in Scorpio, detriment in Taurus, exaltation in Aries (or Pisces), fall in Libra (or Virgo)

After interpreting the building blocks of the horoscope thus far, it's now time to begin to integrate the disparate parts of the chart into a cohesive story of the soul. In the next chapter we'll look at aspects, which are the angled lines that connect all the different parts together.

CHAPTER SIX

The Aspects

ASPECTS ARE THE angles the planets and other cosmic bodies make to each other in the horoscope. Different aspects differ in their angles between the aspected bodies. Aspects tie the disparate elements of the horoscope together to create a cohesive story. It's a highly complex subject that can only be mastered by practice, and one must learn the basics first.

Aspects refer to the distance, in terms of degrees, between points in the horoscope. The horoscope consists of 360° and each aspect is a division of that 360°. For example, the square aspects divide the horoscope by four to make a 90° angle. Like everything in the horoscope, aspects are both yin and yang or day and night. Some are more action-oriented and some are more receptive and connect the other day and night placements.

All aspects create a motivational element and some tension that inspires a person to act. How motivational an aspect is depends on the aspect itself and the elements involved. There are no good or bad aspects, as the less harmonious aspects tend to give more impetus but cause more stress, and the harmonious aspects tend to require conscious effort to be activated but are more easeful. We'll look at this more in future chapters.

Generally speaking, the aspects that divide the chart by an even number are seen as night aspects, as they have to integrate disparate energies, and the aspects that divide the chart by odd numbers are day aspects, which have a more energized way of working together.

The angles that are most important are the Ptolemaic aspects, the conjunction (two planets together), the opposition (180° separation), the square (90° separation), the trine (120° separation), and the sextile (30° separation). I suggest focusing on these the most, especially if you are a beginner. Use the other aspects to create an even more nuanced reading as you grow your practice.

THE CONJUNCTION ☌ 0°

A conjunction is when two planets or other essential bodies are together or within a few degrees of each other in the horoscope. This aspect can be either night or day in tone, which is dependent on the blending of the planetary bodies, sign, and house.

A conjunction is a powerful blending of the two planets or bodies, which both intensifies the symbolism of the two planets and confuses the energies, creating difficulties in seeing the energies of the two separate bodies. The individual planets seem to lose their individuality and take on some of the characteristics of the other, with the outer planet usually having more of an impact on the inner planet. The closer the conjunction, the stronger the merging of the symbolism and the greater the difficulty in separating out and feeling the individual strengths of each planet. It is generally considered a harmonious aspect but is one that requires a more complex understanding of how the symbolism of the planets, sign, and houses work together.

For example, Neptune conjuncting Venus means that the individual may have difficulty seeing those they are in relationships with clearly and will have an ethereal quality to others. They will also often have unrealistic idealism they cannot see within themselves.

THE OPPOSITION ☍ 180°

The opposition is when two planets or other essential bodies are visually opposing each other in the horoscope and are approximately 180° apart. In other words, the 360° of the zodiac is divided by two to create the 180° aspect. Traditionally said to be a disharmonious aspect, the key to working with an opposition in the chart is integration of the opposing energies. This is a night aspect and is an exhalation of breath. To understand how they can work together, it's necessary to blend the symbolism of the planets, signs, and houses.

This is an aspect that has more perspective than the conjunction. The opposing planets can see each other and, therefore, the subject finds it easier to understand how to integrate the two. The two planets communicate and negotiate with each other, which can feel like an inner negotiation that is true of any two differing subjects meeting face to face.

For example, the Moon opposing Jupiter will, at a simple level, give the subject very big highs and lows emotionally, since Jupiter expands and the Moon symbolizes emotions. The sign and house placements will give a deeper understanding.

THE TRINE 120° △

The trine is an aspect in which the planets are approximately 120° apart, which means that the 360° of the zodiac is divided by three. These aspects are almost always in the same element, unless they are dissociated. This is the most flowing and harmonious aspect. The planets work effortlessly together, complementing and enriching. This is a day aspect or inhalation of breath.

The trine shows us where our natural strengths are. The two planets are in signs of the same element and work in a symbiotic relationship. However, since the aspects flow so easily, there is little impetus to consciously embody those strengths. This aspect is an instinctive one but one that can bring a feeling of being truly in alignment when activated.

For example, Venus in Libra trine Neptune in Aquarius means a person is likely to be highly intuitive and creative, but since it comes so naturally, they may not actually utilize that strength in their daily life. Because trines are usually in the same element (in this case air), it often means the subject is not able to bring the impetus of another element to maximize the aspect. When the person becomes aware of this, however, and begins to integrate these strengths into their life, they can fulfill their soul's potential with greater ease.

THE SQUARE 90° □

The most challenging and most energizing aspect is the square, which means that the two planets or other essential bodies are separated by approximately 90°, and the 360° of the zodiac is divided by four. This is a night or exhale aspect.

In a square aspect, the planets are in the greatest tension to each other. The angle of the square suggests that the planets can't see eye to eye and yet are affected by each other. This is said to be a disharmonious aspect, yet it also gives the most impetus to break through the evolutionary blocks and lessons that the aspect requires. The planets are almost vying for preeminence, and yet if the subject can consciously integrate the conflicting energies, this aspect has great power.

For example, Venus square Saturn can indicate blocks in intimacy in relationships and/or frugality with money. With conscious awareness and maturity, the tension can be relaxed and transmuted into stability in a relationship and/or the ability to build great financial success.

THE SEXTILE 60° ✱

The sextile connects two planets that are approximately 60° apart, and the 360° of the zodiac is divided by six. The sextile is an aspect of opportunity that is also considered to be harmonious. The sextile also requires conscious effort to assimilate and embody its potential power, but when activated it opens pathways to growth that can bring great potential. This is sometimes described as a weaker trine, but that description is overly simplistic; with all aspects, the planets, signs, and houses involved change the power of the aspect considerably. This is generally a day or inhale aspect, but consideration of the elements involved must be used.

The sextile is generally an aspect that brings mutual stimulation to both placements, because it usually connects planets in two different elements to create extra stimulus and results.

For example, Mars in Gemini might be sextile to Saturn in Leo and the combination of both Mars (will) and Saturn (determination) in air (Gemini symbolizing communication) and fire (Leo symbolizing leadership) would make for a very strong leader who communicates with authority.

ORBS

An orb is the number of degrees apart from exact that is allowed for each aspect. Orbs are a contentious issue within astrological traditions, and every astrologer has their own view on them. Generally speaking, the Sun and Moon are given a wider orb, as are the Ptolemaic aspects, with the conjunction and opposition being given the widest orbs.

Please take these suggested orbs as a guide. With practice, you will come to find what works for you and understand whether a combination needs to be given a wider orb.

The Conjunction: 10° orb for the luminaries and 8° for other planets

The Opposition: 9° orb for luminaries and 7° for other planets

The Trine and Square: 8° orb for luminaries and 6° for other planets

The Sextile: 4° orb for luminaries and 3° for other planets

The Quincunx, Quintile, Semisquare and Sesquisquare: 3° orb for luminaries and 2° for other planets

The Semisextile: 2° orb for luminaries and 1° for other planets

THE QUINCUNX OR INCONJUNCT 150° ⊼

This is a challenging aspect that involves planets in both different elements and different modalities, so it's difficult to find any common ground between the aspected planets. It's a breakaway aspect

Harmonics

Harmonics are a different way to look at aspects and were developed by John Addey in his 1976 book, *Harmonics in Astrology*. Harmonic horoscopes are based on resonance and overtones that are present in the chart.

To put it briefly, the whole 360° of the zodiac is the basic tone and represents the number one, and the harmonics charts seek to unite planets that work together in a chart. This is a complex calculation that, thankfully, most good astrology software will calculate for you. There are no signs and houses in a harmonics chart, only aspects, and each harmonics chart rearranges aspects that are connected by the number of that harmonic chart, making the aspect connections easier to see.

For example, and put very simply, the fourth harmonic shows how we deal with stress and struggle and unites aspects that divide the zodiac by four, the fifth harmonic indicates talent and unites quintiles and biquintiles, and the seventh harmonic represents inspiration and illusion. Since there can be as many harmonics as there are numbers, I suggest studying this after you gain some mastery of the basics of chart interpretation.

that invites adjustment to understand that the two aspected planets really cannot be integrated in the way an opposition or square can. The two are conflicting because the differences are very complex, and it's necessary to encourage deep awareness and acceptance of an internal drive to compartmentalize the two areas of life so that the subject understands why this need exists.

The discordant nature of this aspect is reflected by the fact that 150° is not a whole-number division of the 360° of the zodiac.

For example, a person with Venus in Leo quincunx or inconjunct Saturn in Capricorn has a love nature that is very playful and joyful and often a desire to be around children, aspecting a need to work hard and build great security. This person will feel torn between the need to play and the need to work and find it difficult to resolve the two, always feeling like they "should" be doing the other, which leads to feelings of guilt.

THE QUINTILE 72° Q

The quintile divides the 360° of the zodiac by five to create a 72° aspect between two planets in the chart and, as such, is a day aspect or an inhale. In a horoscope, a quintile usually denotes creative talent, especially regarding patterns and structures. Those with a quintile or quintiles in their chart are usually more fulfilled in life when they create or find patterns of behavior that make the most of the two aspected planets, because these planets is where the subject is powerfully driven.

A quintile between Mercury and Jupiter, for example, will mean that the person is driven to learn as much as they can, since Mercury is the mind and information and Jupiter is expansion. This person may constantly be reading and/or taking classes.

The Sun can never be quintile to Mercury or Venus, as the three travel too closely together and are never 72° apart.

THE SEMISQUARE ∠ 45°

The semisquare divides the 360° of the zodiac by eight. It is half a square and similar to a square in that it represents a block. Awareness of the block is often activated by external events that invite the subject to work to integrate the two energies. It's often an area of inflexibility and the aspect is actually inviting you to become more flexible and to learn ways to move past blocks. This is a night or exhale aspect.

A semisquare between Mars and Saturn, for example, is one that often brings a tendency to give up when things feel too hard, when you are actually being asked to face your responsibilities and commitments with patience and perseverance in order to move through the block. When that lesson is learned, the person with this aspect can move mountains.

THE SESQUISQUARE ⊡ 135°

This is another minor aspect, the discordant energy of which is reflected by the fact that it doesn't divide the 360° of the zodiac into a whole number. It is also known as the sesquiquadrate. This aspect is, however, a semisquare times three (3 × 45°), or a combination of a square and a semisquare, and this gives an indication of what it symbolizes. I would describe this as a holding of breath, neither inhale nor exhale.

This is another aspect that causes tension and challenge and one that is said to need control, as the two aspected planets often lead to poor choices in life that amplify the lowest symbolism of the two aspected planets.

THE SEMISEXTILE 30° ⋁

The semisextile is an aspect that divides the 360° of the zodiac by 12, which means the aspected planets are in adjacent signs. The suggested orb of 2° for luminaries and 1° for other planets means that this would very rarely be a dissociate or out-of-sign aspect, though it does occur. This aspect has mixed interpretations, with one school positing that since the signs are adjacent and, therefore, of different modalities and elements, it can be a challenge for the planets to work together. However, there are others who believe that the zodiac is ordered the way it is purposefully and that the energy of the signs is of personal growth and evolution, with each sign building off the preceding one. Because of that, this aspect is a helpful one for the soul's evolutionary growth and is a day or inhale aspect.

Both interpretations can be true depending on the level of awareness and consciousness of the subject. A person who is already on the path of personal growth is more likely to be able to integrate the two planets to create opportunities out of any difficulties the two energies bring.

MOST ASPECTED PLANET

The planet that is aspected the most by other planets and essential bodies is important to look at because that planet becomes one of the focal points in the chart, since it's connected to so much else in the chart. This means that any interpretation of the chart must include a close examination of this planet. Much

Dissociate Aspects

Dissociate aspects are also known as "out-of-sign" aspects and can be less easy to spot.

Most aspects are from and to signs of a certain modality or element. For example, a square from a planet in mutable sign Sagittarius will usually involve another planet in Virgo or Pisces, also mutable signs.

However, because of orbs, an aspect can occur in what appears to be the "wrong" sign, and this happens when the aspected planets are in the very last degrees and the very early degrees of signs.

For example, if the Moon is at 28° Sagittarius and Mars is at 1° Aries, they would still be in a square aspect, as they are separated by 93°. An exact square would be 28° Sagittarius to 28° Pisces, and the extra 3° takes the aspect into Aries, but the aspect is still "in orb."

of the client's life will be associated with this focal planet.

The most aspected planet is challenged because the energy of that planet must integrate so many other aspects, but this also makes the planet a powerful focal point for the same reason. The nature of that challenge is symbolized by a synthesis of all the aspects, and it can get very complex.

For example, if Mercury, the planet of learning, is the most aspected planet, great wisdom can be gained by integrating all the wisdom from the planets aspected, but it can also lead to hyperanalysis because there is so much information to integrate. Much of this person's life will be connected to the gathering of information, learning, and communication.

UNASPECTED PLANETS

Unaspected planets are very important. They should always be noted and are usually considered to be those that make no Ptolemaic aspects (conjunction, sextile, square, trine, or opposition) with any other planet.

Unaspected planets represents parts of the self that stand alone and can be a challenge to integrate in life. They can, however, represent an area of great strength or an area of vulnerability and weakness, depending on how the subject responds to the unaspected planet and its other strengths, such as dignity or debilitation. Since unaspected planets can represent both gifts and challenges, both difficult for the person to embody, an understanding of the planet by sign and house can help the person both face those challenges and embody the gifts that planet offers.

An unaspected planet can mean a person feels out of step with and misunderstood by the rest of the world, especially if the unaspected planet is a personal one, like the Sun, the Moon, Mercury, Venus, or Mars.

We have now looked at most of the building blocks of an astrological chart, including the elements, modalities, planets, decans, and aspects, and in the next chapter we'll look at the houses that indicate the areas of life in the chart.

CHAPTER SEVEN

The Houses

THE HOROSCOPE, OR astrological chart, is made up of many elements that must be integrated to create a cohesive blueprint of your soul and your soul's evolutionary potential in this lifetime. We've looked at the planets and other essential bodies, which are the "what" in your blueprint. We've also looked at the signs through the lens of the core self, the Sun, which symbolizes "how" the planets behave in your blueprint.

Now we come to the houses, of which there are 12, running counterclockwise in the horoscope. The horoscope is a combination of the zodiac wheel, which represents the Sun's yearly rotation along the ecliptic from our perspective, and the wheel of houses, which is based on the Earth's 24-hour axial rotation. Accurate birth details, date, time, and place are necessary to create a horoscope, which joins the two wheels together.

The 12 houses symbolize areas of life or fields of experience. This is where the "what" (planets and other essential bodies) and "how" (the signs) work in you and your life. The houses follow a path of personal development from birth (the first house) to death (the 12th house). The houses are also like a pulse or breath of the cosmos, like everything else in the horoscope. For example, the first house, ruled by Aries and Mars, is a day house or inhale, the second is a night house or exhale, and so on.

Adding houses into the interpretation of the horoscope is one of the ways we begin to understand the uniqueness of each cosmic blueprint. A person with the Sun in Sagittarius in the second house will have a different life experience than a person with the Sun in Sagittarius in the 10th house, for example. The former will have more of a core emphasis on personal values and self-worth and the latter will have more of a focus on career and their public life.

THE FIRST HOUSE: THE HOUSE OF SELF

The first house represents birth and early life. It's the first inhalation of life and a day, action-oriented, angular house. The cusp of the first house represents the sign on the eastern horizon at the moment and place of birth in the horoscope as seen from the perspective of that time and place. The first-house cusp is also known as the rising sign, or ascendant, and represents the dawn of a new life itself as the subject takes their first breath when they are born. The first house is ruled by Mars and Aries in the natural horoscope.

This is the house of the self, your life force, and the sign on the cusp or beginning of the house correlates with the ascendant and your persona. The ascendant and first house are your personal receptionist and represent the self or "I am" presence, and it's where you first see yourself before you begin to mature and evolve.

Planets contained within this house will be colored by the sign in the first house and will be directly projected to those you meet: This is how others see you at first. Your early childhood experiences and natural abilities are also represented in the first house, as are your actual birth experience and your spontaneous reactions to outer stimuli.

THE SECOND HOUSE: THE HOUSE OF RESOURCES

The second house is where we exhale and become aware of the physical world, the body, nature, possessions, and money. It's where we establish our connection to the material world. The second house is the realm of matter that we can touch, see, hear, smell, and taste and is a night energy, as we are more receptive to the senses at night. This house is ruled by Venus and Taurus.

This is the realm of all resources, including your inner resources, self-esteem, self-worth, core values, and relationship to the body and the natural world. This is also the realm of what you value, your relationship to money and possessions in the physical realm.

The second house is self-sufficiency and sensuality, which is modified by the planets in and sign on the cusp of the house. Jupiter in the second house, for example, often represents a person with high self-worth and a great ability to make money and they are also likely to love exploring nature.

THE THIRD HOUSE: THE HOUSE OF COMMUNICATION

The third house is where we move into our conscious mind and begin to learn about the world around us. This is a

day, inhale, and cadent house, because in this house we hone our perception and observation skills and gather information. We find our voice in this house, learn to write, and develop our communication styles. This house also represents our early education, learning style, and what kind of school student you are or were, as well as your siblings and neighbors. The third house is where we develop awareness of other points of view and the greater world around us.

This is also the realm of transportation and short journeys, emails, gossip, phone calls, and text messaging, and it is ruled by Mercury and Gemini.

Saturn in the third house, for example, could indicate a diligent student but a person of few words.

THE FOURTH HOUSE: THE HOUSE OF THE HOME

In the fourth house, we exhale again and enter the realm of the night and an angular house as we go within to both our home, as in where we live, and our inner home, the most private part of our inner life. This area of life represents the foundations of our security, both emotionally and materially. Your upbringing is reflected in this house, along with one or both of your parents and ancestral

House Systems

There are at least 50 different house systems, which are a means of dividing the horoscope. Some of the more commonly used systems are those of Porphyry, Placidus, Koch, and Whole Signs. Placidus is the default house system for much of the chart-creation software and became the most popular because there were more tables of houses available when horoscopes were hand drawn.

Astrologers moving toward the Hellenistic revival tend to use Whole Signs, and many evolutionary astrologers use Porphyry—with some having moved to Koch, which is a newer system.

There are many ways to divide space and there's general agreement in many house systems that the horizon, known as the ascendant, starts the first house, the midheaven (zenith) starts the 10th house, and the houses are a division between the angles. My preferred system is Porphyry, which divides the space between the angles by three, the trinity. I do not, however, recommend a system, and I would encourage you to research for yourself to learn over time what you prefer.

influences and patterns. In developmental terms, it's where we become aware of our inner emotional landscape and how we respond emotionally to the world around us.

This house is associated with the Moon and the sign of Cancer. One area of life that is often not mentioned is self-care and self-love. How you were nurtured and how you learn to nurture yourself and fulfill your emotional needs are reflected here, including the type of home you create or prefer.

Someone with Pluto in the fourth house, for example, may have had a difficult childhood with power struggles of some kind within the home and may be driven to transform that in their own life, breaking ancestral patterns.

THE FIFTH HOUSE: THE HOUSE OF SELF-EXPRESSION

The fifth house is a fire house, is associated with the Sun and Leo, and is an inhalation of breath, a day energy, and a succedent house. This is where we develop our creative self-expression and joy in life.

I always think of the fifth house in the soul's development as the teenager, the adolescent, and the place where we begin to shine our light in the world, where we develop our self-consciousness. This is

the realm of children, fun, and *joie de vivre* (French for "joy of life"). It's where we take up hobbies and sports, where we learn to play, and it's the first of the relationship houses because it's where we find love affairs. Your performing ability and your life stage are reflected in the fifth house.

An emphasis in this house would normally indicate someone drawn to the creative arts and someone who approaches the world in a joyful way.

THE SIXTH HOUSE: THE HOUSE OF SERVICE AND HEALTH

The sixth house is associated with Virgo, an earth sign, and is ruled by Mercury. This is a night energy and is an exhale and a cadent house. The sixth house is where we find the need to be useful in the world, to be of service in our daily routines and work. Your day-to-day work experience, nature of work, and style of daily living are represented by this house. Health is also associated with the sixth house, as are your pets.

In developmental terms, the sixth house is where we begin to figure out how we can make a contribution to the world and to others. It's where we begin to change from the inner landscape of personal development and grow into the outer world of adulthood.

The night or exhale energy of the sixth house is a response to the world around us and a desire to create some order in the world. As such, cleansing and hygiene are connected, and your response to all outer stimuli is reflected here.

THE SEVENTH HOUSE: THE HOUSE OF RELATIONSHIP AND MARRIAGE

In the seventh house, our soul takes a big inhale and really enters the realm of the outer or adult world. This house is ruled by Libra and Venus, in her more out-ward, day incarnation, and is a day and an angular house. This house correlates with the descendant, the point opposite the ascendant, which reflects what you are attracted to and what you attract in others.

The seventh house is associated with all significant interpersonal relation-ships, including the main partner or partners in life. This house also includes adult children, significant business or work relationships, and significant friendships. The nature of and the pat-terns in your relationships are reflected in this house. Another area associated with this house is what Jung called the "disowned self," which is a part of the self that we don't like and that we see in others. This can often be seen as something in others that triggers a strong emotional reaction of dislike.

As the second of the relationship houses, the seventh house represents where we join in partnership by either living with or marrying a person. The eighth house builds on this in long-term relationships.

THE EIGHTH HOUSE: THE HOUSE OF INTIMACY AND DEATH

The eighth house is another exhale and a night house, where we are plunged into all things associated with the dark, and is associated with Pluto and Scorpio. This house is a succedent house and is the realm of deeply bonded relationships, the long-term partnership that is con-nected emotionally, psychologically, and sexually. It's the energy of merging of life, resources, and spiritual bodies. This is the third relationship house and where the true intimacy of relationship exists in long-term relationships.

This is also the realm of both physical and psychological death and psycholog-ical transformation and regeneration. Inheritances and other, often taboo, subjects are associated with this area of the horoscope, such as the realms of magic and the occult. This is the realm of deep therapy or soul exploration and your relationship to all shared power and karmic material. Power and powerlessness are the realm of the eighth house, and manipulative and/or abusive power dynamics can show up in this house. This includes your own shadow psychological realms, the parts of you that you may prefer not to look at too closely—though this is also the realm of your inner gold, or buried treasure, so fearless exploration of your eighth house can bring great rewards.

THE NINTH HOUSE: THE HOUSE OF THE HIGHER SELF

The ninth house is another inhale and a day energy, which takes us out into the realms of expansion and exploration of the world and higher learning. This is a cadent house and is ruled by Jupiter and Sagittarius. The ninth house is the area associated with all forms of higher study (formal and informal), philosophy, and personal beliefs. How you experience whatever the divine is for you will be reflected here and, therefore, religion is also associated with this house. This house can be the place of dogma, but generally it is about expanding the mind and consciousness.

Developmentally, the ninth house takes us on a vision quest to seek the meaning of life. In the ninth house we seek truth, freedom, wisdom, and knowledge of natural law, as well as how the world and nature work. The energy of exploration also means that travel is represented in this house, including long journeys of the mind.

THE 10TH HOUSE: THE PUBLIC SELF

The 10th house is the most public part of your chart and yet is an exhale and earth, night energy, where we reflect on how we are seen in the world. This is an angular house and is ruled by Saturn and Capricorn. The 10th house is the nature of our contribution or mission in life, often said to be our career, and hopefully these will be in alignment. Since this is where you are most visible in the world, this house is also associated with your public reputation or status. This is the realm of the wise elder and where we create man-made laws—as opposed to the natural laws explored in the ninth house. It's a place of gravitas, where we build financial and physical security. Duty and responsibility for others are also represented here, as is integrity.

Like the fourth house, this house is also associated with one of the parents—usually the parent who is more out in the world than the other, or who represented authority and your relationship to authority and established society, such as the institutions that govern our world.

Quadrants

The horoscope is divided into four quadrants as well as different hemispheres, and each quadrant has three houses, which are described as angular, succedent, and cadent.

The angular houses are those with an angle (ascendant, Medium Coeli, descendant, or Imum Coeli) on the cusp. The angular houses are ruled by the four cardinal signs—Aries, Cancer, Libra, and Capricorn—and represent action and the beginning of different stages of life experience. The first is the start of self-development, the fourth is the development of consciousness, the seventh is the development of relationships, and the 10th is the development of your public and group consciousness.

The succedent houses are ruled by the four fixed signs—Taurus, Leo, Scorpio, and Aquarius. In these houses, we consolidate that which was begun in the angular houses.

The cadent houses are ruled by the four mutable signs—Gemini, Virgo, Sagittarius, and Pisces. In these houses, we begin to think of the change to come as we move from one phase of development into the next.

THE 11TH HOUSE: THE HOUSE OF COMMUNITY

The 11th house is an inhale of breath, a day, succedent house that takes us out into the community in all its forms and is associated with Uranus and Aquarius. This is the realm of groups of friends, organizations, and associations. The 11th house is also associated with social causes, social consciousness, and politics. A strong emphasis here means the person is likely to be a humanitarian and have an interest in ecology.

Another association for this house is the Internet, due to the community aspect of the house, particularly social media. Latent or undiscovered abilities can also be found here, and the house is associated with the future, big goals, new ideas, and discoveries.

Developmentally, we move from creating solid ambition, rules, and foundations in the world in the 10th house and now move into the realm of making social connections. In this house, we learn to detach from the rules imposed by the authority of the 10th house, to go our own way, and to explore our own realm of genius to create our future.

THE 12TH HOUSE: THE HOUSE OF THE UNCONSCIOUS

In the 12th house, a cadent house, we exhale for the last time on this journey as we enter the night energy of the unconscious. This is the realm of all things mysterious and mystical and is associated with Neptune and Pisces.

This house is the time before birth and the time before death, the amniotic fluid before the first inhale in the first house, the prenatal experience, and the time of fading before the very last exhale. All forms of altered states are represented here, including chemically induced states and meditative states. Creative and intuitive, this house connects us to transpersonal knowledge and understanding. This house is a liminal space, the space between worlds, and is associated with all transitional spaces and activities such as trance, hypnotism, and mysteries.

Seclusion and secluded places are also associated with this house, such as prisons, monasteries, retreat centers, and hospitals. This is a place of dreaming, strong empathy, and the mysterious unknown.

Now that you have the building blocks of an astrology chart, it's time to review and begin to integrate a cohesive story of the self. In the next chapter, we'll look at how each element is involved in the structuring of the birth chart.

UNDERSTANDING YOUR

BIRTH CHART

IN PART 2, we are taking the building blocks we covered in part 1 and moving into considering the birth chart as a whole. This includes structuring and interpreting your birth chart and understanding other celestial bodies.

CHAPTER EIGHT

Structuring Your Birth Chart

IN THIS CHAPTER, I will briefly review the astrological elements of signs, houses, and planets that were discussed in part 1 (see page 1) and go into more detail about how each element is involved in the structuring of the birth chart. Please remember that we are using the concepts of day and night and inhale and exhale to indicate the living, pulsing nature of the cosmos as it works within you.

THE SIGNS

In an astrological horoscope, the outer rim of the chart represents the zodiac, with the belt representing the 12 astrological signs and, like any geometric circle, containing 360°. The medicine wheel or "circle of animals" is divided into 12 equal parts of 30° that are roughly based on, but not equivalent to, the constellations. Most of the planets and other essential bodies move through the signs of the zodiac along the plane of the ecliptic, known as the orbit, in a narrow band. Pluto and some of the newly discovered dwarf planets, however, do not follow the same orbital plane, giving them an orbit that is eccentric compared to the more traditional planets.

The zodiac signs always follow the same order, from Aries to Pisces, going counterclockwise around the outer rim of the horoscope. The signs represent 12 psychological impulses and needs,

HOUSES

See following page for descriptions of each of the 12 sectors that correspond to the numbers in the diagram on the right.

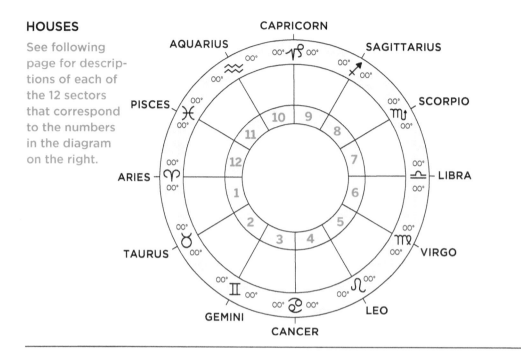

and everyone has all 12 signs contained within their psychological blueprint. In my illustration on this page, the sign on the ascendant, 9:00 on the sample chart, is Aries, but the sign on the ascendant in an individual chart will vary dependent upon time and place of birth. You will see this in the two sample charts at the end of this chapter.

the signs and planets revolve around the ecliptic from our perspective.

Based on the time and place of birth, each house will have a different sign on its cusp, or beginning. Depending on the house system used, some houses may have the same sign on the cusp of two houses. Please see the section on house systems in chapter 7 (see page 65).

HOUSES

Natal charts are divided into 12 sectors, or pieces of the pie, also moving counterclockwise. The houses are fixed, holding the same position in every chart, and the signs revolve around them, just as

PLANETS

Contained within each of the signs and houses are the symbols for the planets and other essential bodies. Each planet represents a part of the psyche that is contained within the whole. The sign it

The Twelve Sectors of the Houses

1

House of the Self

Inhale, Day

Personality

What You Project

Life Force

Early Experiences and Abilities

2

House of Resources

Exhale, Night

Self Confidence, Values

Relationship to Body, Physical World

How You Make Money

3

House of Communication

Inhale, Day

Perception and Observation

The Voice

Writing and Communication Style

Early Education

Siblings, Neighbors

Transportation and Short Journeys

4

House of the Home

Exhale, Night

Inner, Private Life

Emotional and Material Security and Foundation

Fulfillment of Emotional Needs, Self Care

Type of Home

5

House of Self-Expression

Inhale, Day

Creative Expression

Joy, Pleasure, Play, Hobbies

Love Affairs, Romance

Children

6

House of Service and Health

Exhale, Night

Usefulness, Service

Daily Routines and Work

Nature of Daily Work

Health Matters, Cleansing, Daily Diet

Pets

7

House of Relationship and Marriage

Inhale, Day

What You Are Attracted to and What You Attract

Significant Relationships

Disowned Self

8

House of Intimacy

Exhale, Night

Deeply Bonded Relationships

Deep Psychological Issues

Transformation and Death

Inheritances and Shared Financial Resources

9

House of the Higher Self

Inhale, Day

Expansion and Exploration

Higher Studies and Philosophy

Personal Beliefs

Experience of the Divine

Long Journeys and Other Cultures

10

House of the Public Self

Exhale, Night

Contribution or

Mission in Life

Career

Public Visibility and Reputation

One of the Parents

11

House of Community

Inhale, Day

Groups and Organizations

Friends

Social Causes, Consciousness

Humanitarianism

Politics, Including Gender Politics

Internet Connections

12

House of the Unconscious

Mystery, Mystical, Meditation

Altered States, Chemical or Meditative

Transpersonal Knowledge

Seclusion, Retreats, Monasteries, Prison

Dreaming, Empathy

is in represents how that planet is activated, and the house represents the area of life in which the planet is active.

SAMPLE CHARTS

Let's look at some sample natal charts: Jodie Foster and Anderson Cooper.

Jodie Foster

Jodie Foster was born on November 19, 1962, at 8:14 a.m. in Los Angeles, California. The famous actress has the Sun in Scorpio, a Scorpio stellium, the Moon in Virgo, and Sagittarius rising.

I suggest taking an overall view of the chart before delving into the details. This chart is predominant in water elements, with the Sun, Mercury, Venus, Jupiter, and Neptune all in water signs. Her ascendant is in Sagittarius, a fire sign, with Mars in Leo, another fire sign, in aspect, and her Moon, Uranus, and Pluto are in Virgo, an earth sign. This suggests that Foster is predominantly a spiritual, imaginative, and creative soul. Her primary modality is fixed, suggesting she enjoys stability, and her secondary modality is mutable, so she is able to move with changes when needed.

JODIE FOSTER

Natal
Nov 19, 1962, Mon
8:14 AM PST +8:00
Los Angeles, California
Tropical
Porphyry

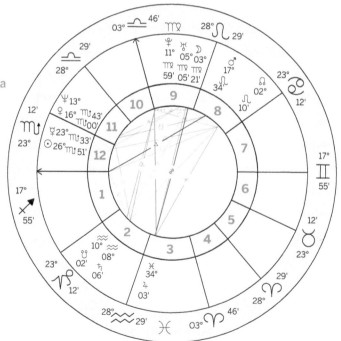

Sagittarius-rising individuals are often drawn to travel and higher learning. Foster has done both, studying in France at a young age, speaking French fluently, and graduating magna cum laude from Yale. The ruling planet of Sagittarius is Jupiter. Foster's Jupiter is in Pisces in the third house, suggesting a very expansive and almost sponge-like ability to learn and take in information. Jupiter opposes the Moon-Uranus-Pluto conjunction in the ninth house (naturally ruled by Sagittarius), which reflects her draw to higher studies, but also that she says she ritualizes all religions in her home so that her family is educated in all belief systems (ninth house). Jupiter in the third house suggests her early academic prowess, and Foster is said to have been able to read at the age of three.

The Sun in a Scorpio stellium that spans the 11th and 12th houses with the luminary in the 12th house shows her intensely private personal nature, as both Scorpio and the 12th house are representative of privacy.

Foster's Mars, traditional ruler of Scorpio, in Leo is in the eighth house, the natural house of Scorpio, which adds to that drive for privacy—though a Leo

A New View of the Planets

Planets are usually named after gods and goddesses from ancient times and mythologies, but remember that the gods represent anthropomorphized parts of the human experience and are archetypal in nature. Similar myths and themes appear in diverse cultures, with different names given to those archetypal representations.

It was humankind who portrayed the gods as masculine or feminine, because of the limits of our understanding, and this has carried through into the language of astrology.

I am not suggesting that we rename the planets, but that we recognize the human lack of nuance imposed on the astrological interpretation of the planets. For example, Mars has been described as masculine for hundreds of years, yet traditionally the planet ruled both Aries and Scorpio, seen as masculine and feminine signs respectively. The planets are as nuanced as human beings. All living beings, including planetary bodies, have both day and night within them—the whole universe is actually nonbinary in nature.

Mars also has the ability to perform. The Libra midheaven also reflects her creative nature, as does her Venus-Neptune conjunction in Scorpio. Her water placements, 8th- and 12th-house placements, and her Jupiter in Pisces suggest a deeply intuitive and possibly psychic nature. They also show a deep desire to explore the psychological motivations of others, and Foster has displayed this through the roles she has chosen and the projects she has directed.

Her Moon-Uranus-Pluto conjunction in Virgo in the ninth house also shows her inclination to explore emotionally deep and psychologically traumatic (Uranus-Pluto conjunction) areas of life. *Taxi Driver* and *The Silence of the Lambs* come to mind in her film roles, and her Yale thesis topic was Toni Morrison, whose writings explore slavery and racism in African American history.

Foster's chart shows a highly intelligent, exploratory nature with a deep sensitivity, intuitive nature, and emotional power that she brings to her public film work and keeps private otherwise.

Anderson Cooper

Anderson Cooper was born on June 3, 1967, at 3:46 p.m. in New York, New York. Cooper's primary element is air, with a Gemini Sun, Libra rising, and Mars in Libra conjuncting the ascendant.

Water is a close second with midheaven, ruling planet Venus, and Neptune all in water signs. The Moon, Jupiter, and Saturn in fire signs are a close third. Cooper's only earth placement is a Uranus-Pluto conjunction in Virgo. Cooper has a good balance of cardinal, fixed, and mutable energy. The majority of Cooper's planets are in the southern hemisphere, or top half, of the chart, suggesting he's outgoing and sociable. First impressions are that he is a well-balanced individual.

With a Gemini Sun, Libra rising with Mars conjunct in Libra, and the ruling planet, Venus, at the top of his chart conjunct the midheaven, it's unsurprising that Cooper has chosen a public role in his career—air signs are connected to the mind, media, and communication. With Mars on his ascendant and his Moon and Saturn in Mars-ruled Aries, and both close to his descendant, he's driven to get ahead and to succeed. His big break in media was self-made (Aries) by faking a press pass to enter Myanmar and selling his own news segments to Channel One, a small news agency.

His strong water element, with Cancer midheaven, the ruling planet Venus in Cancer and angular (conjunct the midheaven), and Neptune in Scorpio, suggests a deeply caring nature, which has motivated his investigative work—he often shows his emotional side on air. He has been quoted as saying, "Yeah, I would prefer not to be emotional and I would prefer not to get upset, but it's hard not to when you're surrounded by brave people who are suffering and in need."

His 12th-house Uranus-Pluto conjunction, however, suggests a deep connection to trauma and indicates trauma in his own life. His brother took his own life in 1988, and Cooper has admitted to becoming desensitized to the horrors of war after reporting on assignment for several years. His eighth-house Sun also suggests that investigative pull toward the underbelly. Thankfully, his strong air and fire placements help balance this out, so he knows when to move to the lighter side of life to bring himself out of the darker places.

His eighth-house Sun also suggests that he's private about his personal life.

Cooper's Libra rising makes him very attractive and appealing in appearance and manner, and his Leo Jupiter in the 10th house gives him star appeal. His Leo Jupiter also is suggestive of his place in American "royalty" as a Vanderbilt heir.

Now that we've looked at the structure of the chart and begun to develop analysis tools through examples, it's time to delve even deeper into chart interpretation and integrate other elements into the chart. In the next chapter, we'll add in other elements, such as some of the asteroids and angles.

ANDERSON COOPER

Natal
Jun 3, 1967, Sat
3:46 PM EDT +4:00
New York, New York
Tropical
Porphyry

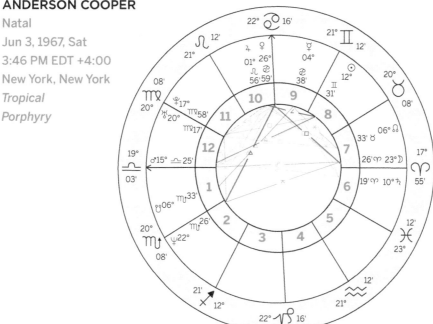

CHAPTER NINE

Interpreting Your Birth Chart

IN THIS CHAPTER, we'll build on all that you have learned so far and introduce some more elements that can add depth to horoscope interpretation. Real insights can be gained from the placement of the Sun, Moon, and ascendant alone, but the insights gained from adding other planets and elements in the chart are invaluable as your knowledge deepens.

In the remaining chapters I'll introduce a few more elements and guide you through a working understanding of how to read your own chart. However, I would like to stress that there is nothing like practice over time to gain deeper insights.

Casting a chart has been made simpler with the advent of astrological computer programs. Before this, you could calculate a chart using a Table of Houses and an ephemeris, but nowadays there are a multitude of options for casting a chart using a computer.

Some of the best professional options are Solar Fire, Matrix, and Astro Gold, but you can calculate a chart for free using Astro.com, one of the best and most comprehensive free options available. Astro Gold has an app, and two other good apps are Time Nomad and TimePassages.

YOUR SUN ☉, MOON ☽, AND ASCENDANT ASC

The Sun, Moon, and ascendant, or rising sign, are the three primary indicators of personality. These should always be considered first as you begin your exploration of a chart. The Sun is your core, the Moon is your soul, and the ascendant is your persona. To accurately calculate the position of all three (and the other elements of the chart), an accurate date, time, and place of birth are necessary. This applies to the Sun particularly if you are born around the 21st of the month, because the Sun moves into the next sign at different days and times every year. Aspects and house cusps are also more accurate with the correct time of birth.

The Sun ☉

As mentioned previously, the Sun is the core essence of who you are. It is your ego, your vital self, the central organizing principle of the solar system and you. Ruled by the heart, the Sun could be said to be the conductor of your orchestra. Life purpose and consciousness is derived from the sign the Sun is in and modified by the house placement and aspects from the Sun to other planets. Those who are living the energy that their Sun placement represents are purposeful and have direction. As a day energy and an inhale of breath, it's who we are when we are taking action in the world, even if the sign you are in is a night or exhale energy. For example, a Cancer Sun will be living a purposeful life when they are nurturing and caring for others. The Sun is the present and the here and now.

The Moon ☽

The Moon represents your soul or innermost core of your being. This is a night or exhale energy, where feelings and needs are primary. The Moon is a subconscious energy that is receptive to all that is around it. It's the response to stress and represents what is needed for comfort and nurture and your basic habits and reactions.

The Moon energy in the chart is instinctive, where you have hunches. How you act on your intuition and hunches consciously is through the Sun. The Moon energy is creative, sentimental, and adaptable and can be protective or moody and irrational, but how that energy expresses itself is dependent on the sign and house placement of the Moon. Again, an accurate time of birth is important to know the exact position of the Moon, especially because the Moon is the fastest moving energy in the chart.

The phase of the Moon you were born under also has some influence. A phase

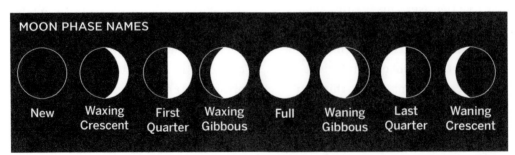

MOON PHASE NAMES

New — Waxing Crescent — First Quarter — Waxing Gibbous — Full — Waning Gibbous — Last Quarter — Waning Crescent

is an angular relationship or aspect between the Sun and Moon in the chart. In brief, if you were born with the Sun and Moon in conjunction, you were born under a new-moon phase (day, inhale, and 0–45°), which is suggestive of a self-starter who wants to shine their light on the world. The waxing-crescent phase (night, exhale, 45–90°) is one who is learning independence and letting go of old patterns. The first-quarter phase (day, inhale, 90–135°) is someone who likes to take action and thrives on change. The waxing-gibbous phase (night, exhale, 135–180°) is someone who has a thirst to receive knowledge in the search for truth.

Full-moon (day, inhale, 180–225°) people have the intense light of the Sun shining on the feelings, so they are often impulsive and instinctual. The disseminating or waning-gibbous phase (night, exhale, 225–270°) is someone who loves to share their knowledge and wisdom with the world. Someone born under the last-quarter phase (day, inhale, 270–315°) is a person who feels somewhat out of step with the world and needs to develop a relationship with their intuitive self. The final, balsamic, or waning-crescent phase (exhale, night, 315–360°) is someone who is deeply sensitive and intuitive.

THE FOUR ANGLES OF THE BIRTH CHART

The four angles of the chart are formed by the intersection of the horizontal and vertical axes of the chart and occur at four points: north, south, east, and west. These are known as the ascendant, descendant, Medium Coeli (MC), and Imum Coeli (IC).

The Ascendant or Rising Sign ASC

The ascendant is the sign and degree that is on the eastern horizon at the moment and place of birth or the start of any event. The rising sign represents the part of you that you present to the world, your "receptionist" that projects a certain image when others meet you. It's the outer layer of being known as the persona, also described as the mask that only reveals what is wanting to be seen initially.

The ascendant also reveals much about a person's birth and early childhood and, as such, the ascendant can sometimes be a defense mechanism in early life and in challenging situations. However, we tend to grow into our ascendant and live it more proactively as we age. For example, a person with Capricorn rising can be very serious and reserved when young but tends to loosen up as they age.

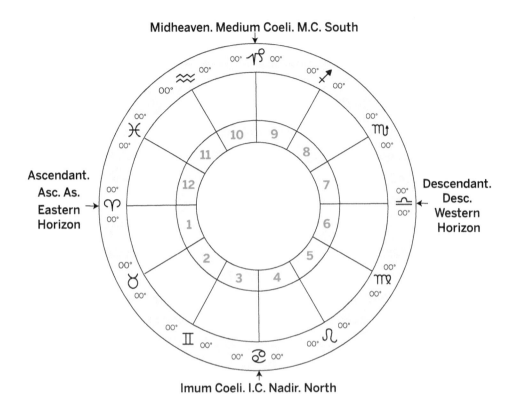

Midheaven. Medium Coeli. M.C. South

Imum Coeli. I.C. Nadir. North

The Medium Coeli (Midheaven)

The midheaven, also known as the Medium Coeli or MC, is the highest point of the chart and is the cusp of the 10th house in most house systems. In the northern hemisphere it represents the south and in the southern hemisphere it represents the north.

The midheaven is the most public place of the chart and represents the mission, goal, or contribution in life. Often said to represent the career, this is not always the case—though it does represent the nature of the career the person would ideally pursue. As the most public place of the chart, this also represents public reputation and social standing.

The Descendant

The sign and degree on the western horizon at the time of birth, the descendant represents what you are attracted to in others and how you relate to other important people in your life. The sign on the descendant represents the energy of those you will seek partnership with in life. If you have Gemini on the descendant, for example, you will enjoy intellectually based partnerships that are a lot of fun. That doesn't necessarily mean Gemini sun sign but rather someone who has a lot of air energy in their chart, including Gemini.

The Imum Coeli (Nadir)

The nadir, also known as the Imum Coeli or IC, is at the very bottom of the chart and represents the north in the northern hemisphere and the south in the southern hemisphere. This is the most private part of the astrology chart and represents your inner, most private life. The sign on the nadir is the cusp of the fourth house in most house systems and also represents one of the parents, usually the one who was most inclined to nurture. The childhood home and the home the person prefers are also represented by the nadir.

CALCULATING ASPECTS

Aspects are a cornerstone of modern horoscope interpretation. For more detail on the different aspects, please see chapter 6 (see page 55).

In order to calculate aspects, you need to know the degree and sign of

Evolutionary Astrology

In most modern western astrological traditions, the birth chart is seen a map of the soul's evolutionary potential and development. The chart is also known as the horoscope, soul map, cosmic blueprint, and natal chart.

In this book, therefore, we are not looking at the chart as a mere description of personality that is unchanging throughout a lifetime, but as a blueprint rich in meaning and possibility. That development occurs through both the planetary transits and cycles and the free will of the person to follow the call of development and evolution. This removes much of the fatalistic interpretations of other astrological traditions.

Predictive astrology has its place, of course. By no means do I mean to suggest that this evolutionary approach is more valid. The evolutionary approach merely suits the nature of this book, as it takes us into a nonbinary approach that works for everyone. In other words, we are talking about both the evolutionary intention of the soul and the evolution of astrology itself.

the planets and the number of degrees between them. The degrees and sign placements of the planets and other bodies can be found using an ephemeris, but luckily we have computer programs that do this for us (see page 85 for suggestions).

PLANETS IN THEIR DOMINION

If a planet is in its home sign, then its strength is intensified, as are the qualities of both sign and planet—whether positive or negative.

For example, Mercury in Gemini would give a more voracious appetite for learning and would also suggest that the person is highly social, dependent on all the other factors in the chart.

RULING PLANET

The planet that is said to rule the chart and the person or event is the planet that rules the sign on the ascendant. The sign and house that this planet is in will modify the ascendant energy. For example, if someone has Aquarius rising and their ruling planet, Uranus, is in Libra in the sixth house, then it would suggest that the person has a unique and even quirky mode of creative self-expression.

STELLIUM

A stellium is three or more planets in a particular sign, meaning the person will be more of that sign than if there is only one planet in the sign. Because Mercury and Venus move with the Sun for much of the Solar year, stelliums will often include one or both of these two personal planets.

PLANETS IN MUTUAL RECEPTION

Two planets are in mutual reception when each one is in the sign that the other one rules. When planets are in mutual reception, they are connected even if there is no aspect between them. The two planets support each other but the quality of that support is dependent on the strength of each planet in the sign in the chart by triplicity, exaltation, detriment, or fall.

For example, if Mars is in Sagittarius and Jupiter is in Aries, both planets are in a fire triplicity sign and, therefore, would support each other well.

ASTEROIDS AND CHIRON

In this section, we'll look at the four main asteroids and Chiron—though Ceres has now been promoted to dwarf-planet status. Ceres is the only body in the asteroid belt so far to be promoted to a dwarf planet. Astronomical definitions of cosmic bodies are changing due to new discoveries; these changing definitions seem only fitting as we move into a new paradigm and begin to change the language used in astrology.

Chiron ⚷

Chiron is one of the most interesting and unusual bodies in astrology. In mythology, Chiron was a centaur, but he was unlike the other centaurs, who were quite base creatures. Most centaurs had a human head and torso and the tail and legs of a horse, but Chiron had human front legs, showing a more human quality. Chiron was a teacher, healer, and archer, and he was immortal. When wounded by a poisoned arrow, his immortality kept him living in agony until he gave up his immortality to save Prometheus.

Because of the myth, Chiron is known as the wounded healer in astrology and it's said that he represents the wound in the chart. If we look at the symbol for Chiron, however, it's shaped like a key. Combined with the nature of the myth and Chiron's reputation as a teacher, mentor, and healer, it's more reasonable to see him as the key to healing in your chart. Chiron is also known as the rainbow bridge between spirit and matter and the maverick shaman.

Chiron doesn't have rulership of a sign, but it is associated with the constellations Centaurus and Sagittarius and has many Sagittarian qualities—though some also associate the centaur with Virgo because of its healing abilities. An unhealthy expression of Chiron would be to focus on the wound rather than the potential healing.

Someone with Chiron in Aquarius in the second house, for example, may be born with a tendency to feel alienated from others, and that may affect self-esteem. However, seeking out higher knowledge and communion with the whole universe will give the person the ability to see the bigger picture of their place within humanity.

Ceres ⚳

Ceres is known as the Great Mother, the goddess of agriculture, and is associated with the signs Cancer, Virgo, and Taurus. In the astrological chart, Ceres represents how we nurture and how we meet our own needs as shown by the sign Ceres is in. The house placement shows what type of experiences will help you promote feelings of self-love and self-acceptance. This equates to your love language.

Ceres is also associated with natural cycles, such as those of pregnancy and birth, the growing cycles, the seasons, and hospices.

When you are living the best expression of your Ceres, you are attuned to the natural cycles of nature and your body and honoring your own love language.

For example, a person with Ceres in Capricorn in the first house feels heightened self-worth when accomplishing personal goals and when helping others be responsible for themselves, but they may also overidentify with responsibility for teaching others and with the need to impress others. When they focus more on their inner accomplishment and less on the need to control how others take responsibility, they are expressing the higher qualities of their Ceres.

Pallas Athena ♀

Pallas Athena is the goddess of wisdom and a warrior whose astrological glyph represents the warrior spear of justice in her role as protector of the state. She is associated with the signs of Libra, Leo, and Aquarius. Pallas Athena represents one's capacity for creative wisdom and original thought, which creates new possibilities. In the chart, she represents inspired vision and the ability to make sense of complex patterns. A strong placement for Pallas Athena is often found in the charts of astrologers, so she is known as the "astrologer's asteroid." I have Pallas Athena exactly conjuncting my ruling planet, Jupiter. Pallas Athena is also known for the soul's desire to

move toward a less binary world and androgyny, so it is apt that I am writing a book that moves beyond the binary world that has dominated astrology. My Pallas Athena not only rules my Sagittarius rising sign, it's also in Sagittarius conjuncting the ruler of Sagittarius, the teacher.

Where your Pallas Athena is, by sign and house, will indicate where and how you are able to utilize creative intelligence.

Vesta ⚶

Vesta is the eternal flame that burns within each of us. In mythology, she was the priestess of the flame and goddess of the Vestal Virgins and is associated with the signs Virgo and Scorpio. Remember that the original meaning of the word virgin was "one who is whole unto themselves," which gives a major indication of the symbology of Vesta in astrology.

Vesta represents focus and commitment. Where the asteroid is by sign and house indicates where we focus our energies or what we are devoted to. An unhealthy expression can suggest fanaticism and obsession rather than focus.

If a person has Vesta in Scorpio in the 10th house, for example, they may be deeply focused on their mission in life and tend to overcommit to that, often to the exclusion of their interpersonal relationships, especially if they are not aware of that tendency.

Juno

Juno was the divine consort, wife of Jupiter (Hera in Greek mythology). In astrology the asteroid Juno represents our capacity for meaningful relationships and is associated with the signs Libra (significant relationships) and Scorpio (deeply bonded relationships).

The sign of Libra is also associated with justice and, as such, Juno is also representative of the oppressed and underprivileged.

Where Juno is found in sign and house placements represents what you most desire in a relationship. In Sagittarius and the 11th house, for example, you would require mutually shared beliefs and vision of the future, and also for the partner to be a friend as well as a lover.

CHAPTER TEN

Taking a Closer Look

IN THIS CHAPTER, we'll delve into some of the finer points of birth-chart interpretation. These include such things as hemisphere emphasis, the Moon's nodes, the Part of Fortune, retrograde planets, intercepted signs, and transits. Of these, the first two are the most important in natal-chart analysis. Transits are a predictive technique and one we are only able to touch on in the scope of this book.

HEMISPHERE EMPHASIS

The astrological chart is divided into four separate hemispheres by the horizon, or horizontal axis, and the meridian, or vertical axis. In this section, we'll look at all four of the hemispheres and what an emphasis of planets and other essential bodies in each hemisphere means.

Southern Hemisphere

The southern hemisphere is the upper half of the chart—this is generally more extroverted and objective and is day or inhale energy.

Those with a larger number of planetary bodies in this hemisphere are likely to lead a conscious, event-oriented life and are likely to be energized by interaction with the outside world.

The house emphasis must be combined with the hemisphere emphasis because the extroverted qualities of the chart will be most apparent if most of the planets are in the seventh, ninth, 10th, and 11th houses, and less marked with a concentration of planets in the eighth and 12th houses, as these two houses are very private areas of life that are night or exhale energy and ruled by water signs, meaning that they are more introverted than the other houses.

Northern Hemisphere

The lower half of the astrological chart is the northern hemisphere. A concentration of planets here means night, exhale energy and a more introverted nature. This is a more subjective and inward-focused person who leads a more intuitive and receptive life.

This person is likely to enjoy solitude and need alone time in order to feel energized. Likewise, too much time around others will be draining.

A concentration in the first and fifth houses will lessen these qualities slightly, as these two houses are more outgoing in outlook.

Eastern Hemisphere

In the astrological chart, the eastern hemisphere is the left side of the chart—an emphasis here is more day, inhale energy. A person with a concentration of planets here is self-determined, goal-oriented, and intentional. These individuals are more likely to use their will to consciously choose and create their own reality. They are often seen as willful and less likely to work well in collaboration with others.

Western Hemisphere

The western hemisphere is the right side of the astrological chart. This is night, exhale energy, where we are more likely to surrender to the will of others and to forces beyond the conscious realm. These individuals are more collaborative and cooperative in nature but are also more likely to be receptive to peer pressure.

As they are the type of person to go with the flow, they find it easier to change

course even if they have consciously chosen a certain path.

THE MOON'S NODES: NORTH ☊ AND SOUTH ☋

The nodes of the Moon are the two points where the Moon's orbit intersects with the ecliptic. The north node is where the Moon crosses the ecliptic in a northerly direction from our perspective and the south node is where the Moon crosses in a southerly direction. The two lunar nodes are always opposing each other.

In most astrological interpretations, the Moon's nodes represent a path of development for the soul in each lifetime, with the south node representing the past and the north, the future. Also known as the dragon's tail (south node) and dragon's head (north node), they also represent our default emotional reactions, or soul habit, and the soul's potential, or habits to consciously move toward. They are a continuum of development, with neither the south node being all bad nor the north node being all good. A brief summary of the meaning of the nodes is as follows:

North Node in First House or Aries: Develop independence, courageousness, spontaneity, and self-awareness

North Node in Second House or Taurus: Develop strong values, self-worth, connection with the Earth and the senses, patience, and loyalty

North Node in Third House or Gemini: Develop curiosity, listening skills, openness to new ideas and other perspectives, and tact

North Node in Fourth House or Cancer: Develop empathy, the ability to notice and validate feelings, humility, and awareness and acceptance of others' feelings and moods

North Node in Fifth House or Leo: Develop self-confidence, creative self-expression, willingness to stand out, and a sense of playfulness and fun

North Node in Sixth House or Virgo: Develop a sense of service, more focus on routines and detail, moderation, and compassionate action

North Node in Seventh House or Libra: Develop the ability to collaborate, diplomacy, awareness of the needs of others and how to live and work with others, and sharing

North Node in Eighth House or Scorpio: Develop less attachment to material worth, awareness of others' psychological desires and motives, and sharing power dynamics

North Node in Ninth House or Sagittarius: Develop awareness of and trust in your intuition or guidance from source, sense of adventure and self-trust, and awareness of higher consciousness

North Node in 10th House or Capricorn: Develop self-control and respect, taking the mature role in situations, responsibility, and dependence on self

North Node in 11th House or Aquarius: Develop self-approval and a willingness to share inventive and unconventional ideas, the ability to work in groups and to connect with humanity in an egalitarian and humanitarian way, and the ability to connect with like-minded people

North Node in 12th House or Pisces: Develop compassion, trust in and surrender to source or the collective creation principle, unconditional love, and a spiritual path and self-reflective practices

South Node in First House or Aries: Work to lessen the grip of the habits of impulsiveness, unhealthy selfishness, anger issues, and overassertiveness

South Node in Second House or Taurus: Work to lessen stubborn tendencies, resistance to change, overattachment to ownership and accumulation of material possessions, overeating, and other overindulgences

South Node in Third House or Gemini: Work to lessen the impact of indecisiveness, the belief that you always need more information or more study before acting, ignoring intuition, and trusting others' opinions and ideas over your own

South Node in Fourth House or Cancer: Work to lessen dependence on others, insecurity, manipulative use of emotions, risk avoidance, and overattachment to fears and safety

South Node in Fifth House or Leo: Work to lessen the need for other's adulation and approval, sense of entitlement, risk-taking, and melodramatic tendencies

South Node in Sixth House or Virgo: Work to lessen the tendencies to be giving to the point of self-sacrifice, difficulties receiving from others, analysis paralysis, anxiety and worry, and being overly critical

South Node in Seventh House or Libra: Work to lessen the habits of selflessness, playing nice to the detriment of yourself and others, codependence, and only being able to see the self through the eyes of others

South Node in Eighth House or Scorpio: Work to lessen obsessive or compulsive habits, preoccupation with the motivations and actions of others, hyperreactivity and irritation with others, and attraction to crisis situations

South Node in Ninth House or Sagittarius: Work to lessen the habits of being dogmatic and self-righteous, not listening to what others are really saying, and talking over others and speaking before thinking things through

South Node in 10th House or Capricorn: Work to lessen the need to be in control of and responsible for everything and everyone, needing to appear strong at all times, and being too goal-focused

South Node in 11th House or Aquarius: Work to lessen the habit of detaching from emotional situations and appearing cold, avoiding confrontation, and tending to shapeshift to fit in with the crowd so you feel accepted rather than embracing your individuality

South Node in 12th House or Pisces: Work to lessen oversensitivity and playing victim, tendencies to withdraw and give up easily, extreme escapism and avoidance of the "real" world, and self-doubt

THE PART OF FORTUNE ⊗

The Part, or Lot, of Fortune is a point that is calculated from the longitudes of the Sun, Moon, and ascendant, a technique that was commonly used in ancient astrology. It is being revived with the resurgence of Hellenistic astrology. It's one of many Arabic or Greek techniques but is the most commonly known and used. The Part of Fortune can be calculated in most astrological software.

The Part of Fortune is calculated by the following method: In a day chart, which is a chart where the Sun is found in the southern hemisphere or above the horizon, the Part of Fortune is found where the Moon would be if the Sun were on the ascendant. In a night chart, where the Sun is found in the northern hemisphere or below the horizon, the Part of Fortune is found where the Sun would be if the Moon were on the ascendant. In both cases, you count the number of degrees between the Sun and Moon and calculate that same distance either clockwise or counterclockwise, depending on the natal-chart placements from the ascendant, to find the placement of the Part of Fortune.

The Part of Fortune generally indicates what the name suggests and shows

Lunar Node Facts: Eclipses and Soul Groups

When a new or full moon occurs near the lunar nodes, from our perspective, eclipses occur.

A lunar (full-moon) eclipse occurs when the Earth comes between the Sun and Moon and within 11° 38' of either lunar node. A solar (new-moon) eclipse occurs when the Moon comes between the Earth and the Sun within 17° 25' of either lunar node. The closer the degree aspect to the nodes, the higher the totality of the eclipse.

The lunar nodes stay in two signs of the zodiac—the south node in one sign and the north node in the opposite or polarity sign—for approximately a year and a half. All eclipses during that period will be in one of the two signs.

Anyone born during that period will share the same nodes, and since the nodes represent a path of soul development, those people are said to belong to the same soul group.

The cycle of the lunar nodes is approximately 18.5 years, so those born around 18.5 years after us will be born into that same group. Those born approximately nine years before or after us are our nodal opposites and we often feel a strong attraction to those people, as they help us develop those north-node traits.

where you may find your luck and how easily you find abundance or wealth. The sign and house that the Part of Fortune is in suggests the area where you will find fortune. For example, a Part of Fortune in Gemini in the sixth house might indicate fortune through speaking or writing, especially if done with a focus on serving others.

RETROGRADE PLANETS

A planet is said to be retrograde when it appears to go backward from our earthly perspective. No planet actually does go backward; the retrograde motion is because of a relative difference in speed when planets are at their closest point to the Earth. When a planet is farther away from the Earth, it appears to be moving direct or forward. In fact, all planets in our solar system are revolving around the Sun, so this anomaly is from our perspective because of our relative orbits.

The days where a planet appears to stop and go retrograde, or direct at the end of the retrograde period, are called the stations. The Sun and Moon never appear to be retrograde. All the other planets do go retrograde and Mercury goes retrograde three or four times a year. In an astrology chart, a retrograde planet either will have red text or will have an "R" next to it. A stationary planet

will have an "S" next to it. Retrograde periods are at their strongest in the lead up to and for a few days after the station date.

The impact of the apparent retrograde is because of the proximity to the Earth and the fact that the planet appears to retrace an area of the zodiac from our perspective, making its energy more keenly felt. The retracing of the path through an area of the zodiac takes us on a more inward or night journey, or invites us to exhale and release some lessons from the period when the planet was direct.

If a natal chart has retrograde planets, then you are likely to feel somewhat out of step with what's considered the norm in society in that area of life—you march to the beat of your own drum. It's also an area where you are more inwardly focused. This is heightened when the retrograde planet is a personal planet, like Mercury, Venus, or Mars. If Jupiter or Saturn is retrograde, the person may feel alien to the dominant culture in some way. If an outer planet—Neptune, Uranus, or Pluto—is retrograde, then the person may feel out of step with their generation in some way. It's uncommon to have more than three retrogrades in a natal chart but if a person does they will feel very out of step with the world they were born into and are likely to be one who really is unique.

INTERCEPTED SIGNS

Intercepted signs occur when using unequal house systems such as those of Placidus, Porphyry, or Koch (see page 67), which are time-based house systems—the first house begins with the actual degree of the ascendant and houses are of different sizes, as they are calculated by dividing the space around the ecliptic by different methods. In these house systems, the difference in size is greater the further away from the equator the person was born. Most modern western astrologers use time-based house systems. Opposing houses are always the same size, so you will always have at least two intercepted signs if you have any. This will also mean that the same sign will rule the cusp of two houses.

Astrologers practicing more traditional techniques often use space-based systems, such as Whole Sign or Equal House systems, where the houses are equally divided by 30°.

When a sign is intercepted in the natal chart, the energy of that sign is harder to access by the person, and it will represent blocks where they have found that part of themselves hard to develop in early life—they will have to consciously learn to develop it. Looking at the placement and aspects of the ruling planet of the intercepted sign can help you learn to access that part of the chart.

Retrograde Explained

All planets have retrograde periods. However, the Sun and Moon never appear to go retrograde. All planets appear retrograde for different periods and with different regularity, known as the synodic period.

MERCURY appears to be retrograde three and sometimes even four times a year and is retrograde for 21 days every 3.8 months.

VENUS appears to be retrograde for around 21 days every 19.2 months.

MARS appears to be retrograde for around 72 days every 25.6 months.

JUPITER appears to be retrograde for around 121 days every 13.1 months.

SATURN appears to be retrograde for around 138 days every 12.4 months.

URANUS appears to be retrograde for around 151 days every 12.15 months.

NEPTUNE appears to be retrograde for around 158 days every 12.07 months.

PLUTO appears to be retrograde for around 150 days every 12.3 months.

ASTROLOGICAL TRANSITS

Transits are a means of interpreting the ongoing movement of the planetary bodies as they relate to the natal chart. A planet can transit a natal planet by any aspect and are a way to forecast trends and personal development. Interpreting a transit involves blending the keywords for the transiting planet by sign and house with the transited planet or point in the chart by sign and house.

One of the most important ways of looking at transits is to look at planetary returns. This means the planet returns to the same point it was at in the natal chart, and this usually only happens for the planets up to Uranus, since Neptune has a 164-year cycle and Pluto has a 248-year cycle.

Lunar returns occur around every 28 days and solar returns occur every 365 days. A return chart can be cast for any planetary return and signifies the person's development and focus for the next cycle of that planet.

The most commonly used return chart is the Solar Return chart. This is cast for the moment the Sun returns to the degree and minute it was at in the natal chart. Astrologers differ as to whether to use the natal place of birth or the current location; I prefer to use the natal. The Solar Return chart is read like the natal chart but is focused only on the coming year. The chart, therefore, is an indicator of what your next solar year will bring and where your focus will be.

One of the best-known returns is the Saturn return, which occurs around the ages of 29, 58, and 87 and indicates major periods of maturation or stages of life.

Now that we have taken a closer look and have added depth to chart analysis, we'll move on to look at your calling, to give you an idea of what careers are a good fit for each sign of the zodiac.

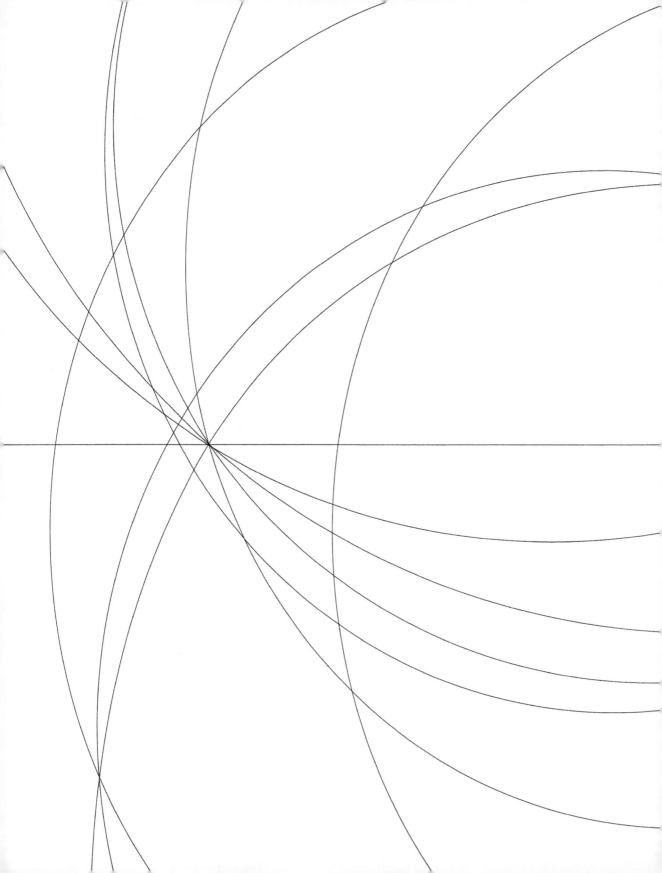

SUN SIGNS AT WORK AND
IN LOVE

IN PART 3, we'll cover all 12 sun signs in work and love to give you some ideas for potential careers and how compatible each sign is with others.

PART

3

CHAPTER ELEVEN

Your Calling According to the Zodiac

A BIRTH CHART can give a person a great indication about the type of work that will be most fulfilling and will best complement a person's unique talents and abilities. It cannot, however, tell you exactly what career path to take, so it's best to see it as the opening up of possibilities.

In this chapter, we'll take a close look at ideal careers and personal profiles as they relate to those careers for each sign of the zodiac. There will be suggested careers for each sign, but please use them as a springboard to other possibilities. For example, a photographer might be a suggestion based on the career indicators in the chart, such as a Gemini midheaven, but if the chart has a heavy eighth-house emphasis as well, the person might be drawn to boudoir photography due to the deeper themes and soul challenges of that style of photography.

To get a clear picture of the career best suited for you, you must look beyond your sun sign—I suggest looking at the sign on the midheaven or cusp of the 10th house in the natal chart and then looking at the sign and house placement of the ruler of that sign to give a deeper picture of what kind of work would suit you best. A deeper reading would also look at the sixth house, to see what daily type of work would suit your personality best, alongside element and modality emphasis, stelliums in a sign, and aspects. In other words, the whole chart must be considered to get an in-depth vocational analysis. In that vein, I will give examples of famous sun-sign individuals—but we are more than our sun sign alone, so please take all of this into account when interpreting your own chart.

ARIES AT WORK

Aries are best suited to careers where they take the lead or work independently, preferably starting new projects with others to whom they can delegate to finish what they started. Aries like fast-moving and competitive environments where their natural enthusiasm will not be dampened. Aries are usually bold and up for any challenge, prepared to take risks, and have a no-nonsense attitude. They are the fearless straight shooters of the world.

Firefighter, surgeon, emergency medical technician, art director, public relations professional, military or law enforcement officer, entrepreneur, venture capitalist, free climber, tour guide, CrossFit instructor or sports coach, athlete, metal sculptor, mechanic, hunter, silver- or other metalsmith, and chef would all be ideal careers for an Aries.

The Aries boss can be inspiring, energetic, and a born leader. You will be left with no doubt how the boss feels about your work, whether that be the highest praise or the rudest and most direct criticism. There is no vindictiveness; the Aries boss is just direct to a fault. The Aries boss dislikes overthinking and expects everyone to put a lot of energy into their work and to complete projects quickly. They also enjoy admiration and respect but can see through any fake flattery in an instant.

Aries employees can be the hardest working and most dynamic employees if you don't try to keep them in a rigid routine or stuck at a desk. If your Aries employees feel bored, they will probably move on. They work best when they are given autonomy and are answerable to as few people as possible. If given the freedom to take ownership of their own schedule and way of working, they will be the most productive and dynamic employees.

The Aries coworker isn't really the best at coworking unless you are happy to let them take the lead and do their own thing. They are competitive and like to be first, so they will not react well if their coworkers make their way up the ladder before they do. However, if you are happy to let them lead, they can be full of zest and very inspiring.

Well-known Aries People

Lady Gaga, Elton John, Tommy Hilfiger, and Jackie Chan were all born under the sign of Aries.

TAURUS AT WORK

Taurus are best suited to careers that give them stability and security. Taurus individuals are loyal and tenacious but can also be stubborn and ponderous. They also love the good things in life: good food, beautiful and comfortable surroundings, and nature.

Taurus love the tangible things of life and, therefore, love to work with the tangible. This means things that they can touch, see, smell, hear, and taste.

Good careers for Taurus are banker, cashier, financier, mortgage officer, singer, farmer, real estate professional, interior designer, podiatrist, reflexologist, florist, gardener, landscaper, jeweler, beauty blogger, brand ambassador, wine maker, chef, landscape photographer, executive assistant, and restaurant manager.

The Taurus boss is a builder and will persistently expand and grow whatever business or field they work in. They are probably the most patient boss of all and they like a harmonious and peaceful environment. As such, they are usually not reactive over small issues. Really big issues, however, can turn the Taurus into a raging bull, but the Taurus boss will usually give the employee a chance to rectify mistakes before losing their cool.

Since the Taurus boss likes solidity and stable outcomes, they usually will be tolerant of those needing extra

Astrological Signs of the Rich and Famous

Reading the Forbes top 100 list of highest paid entertainers for 2018, it's fun to look at which signs best combine talent and wealth-building abilities.

Taurus celebrities topped the list with 12.68 percent of the top 100 born under the sign. This is not surprising, since Taurus natives are usually good at wealth building. George Clooney, Dwayne "The Rock" Johnson, and Jerry Seinfeld are included in this list.

Sagittarians are the least likely entertainers to be included on the list with only 2.7 percent in the top 100. Sagittarians tend to value experience over money, and that may be why there are fewer on the list. Scarlett Johansson and Jay-Z are two of the Sagittarians on the list.

On the Forbes list of billionaires, there were 27 Librans topping the list. Librans are usually very good in business. Ralph Lauren and Alice Walton are included here.

Perhaps surprisingly, since Capricorn is generally an ambitious and hardworking sign, only eight billionaires were born under the sign of Capricorn. Jeff Bezos is on this list.

time to do something well rather than demand it be completed in a rush. They love employees who are disciplined and careful in their approach.

The Taurus employee is reliable, steadfast, and trustworthy. They have a soothing presence around the workplace and don't get thrown off by crisis—in fact, a crisis can bring out the best in them as they calmly deal with a situation.

The Taurus coworker is also pleasant to be around, though their ponderous pace can frustrate some faster moving people, as can their resistance to change. However, they are likely to bring good snacks into the workplace, so if you would like a treat, they are good to connect with. They are also fabulous at helping self-starters finish projects.

Well-known Taurus People

George Clooney, Stevie Wonder, Dwayne "The Rock" Johnson, Kenan Thompson, Sam Smith, and Kristen Stewart were all born under the sign of Taurus.

GEMINI AT WORK

The chatty, curious, and mercurial nature of Gemini means that that they are best suited to careers that give them lots of opportunities to keep learning new information and meeting with lots of people. They are not lovers of routine or sitting still for long. Geminis are persuasive, generally great speakers, youthful, and love multitasking. They enjoy fast-paced environments.

Careers that would suit Gemini individuals are scientist, advertising agent, journalist, writer, teacher, accountant, computer programmer, engineer, project manager, media analyst, communications specialist, interpreter, transportation worker, driver, storyteller, entertainer, radio or podcast host, blogger, photographer, tutor, guide, personal assistant, salesperson, or TV host.

A Gemini boss can be difficult to work for due to their restless and unpredictable nature. They will constantly be on the move. They work best when all routine tasks are delegated, and they are left to deal with ideas and abstract projects and schemes. Change is a constant with the Gemini boss and they tend to notice everything that's going on.

Gemini bosses are hugely likeable, however, as they have a great sense of humor and are very gregarious—but they are generally quite emotionally detached and won't want to get too involved in any emotional dramas among employees. To more staid employees, working for a Gemini boss can feel like a ball of confusion, but they are not the confused ones. If you can live with the changeability and fast pace, you will have fun with this boss.

A Gemini employee does not like being confined in any way and will become very agitated if they feel hemmed in, which will make them ineffective. Although they seem to be absentminded, they really do soak up information and will get the job done. This is especially true if their natural skills are utilized. They are also likely to negotiate raises easily, as they will always have a good argument as to why they deserve it.

As a coworker, Gemini will be a lot of fun—but very distracting, as their mind flits from one subject to another often. They will talk circles around everyone they work with but will be the life and soul of the workplace and will probably organize work parties or events.

Well-known Gemini People

Marilyn Monroe, Paul McCartney, Harvey Milk, Venus Williams, Aung San Suu Kyi, Laverne Cox, and Boy George were all born under the sign of Gemini.

CANCER AT WORK

Cancer individuals are adaptable and a nurturing presence. They are best suited to careers involving looking after people or homes in some way. They are also traditional and love anything to do with heritage and sentiment. Their emotional connection to their career is important, or they are likely to become emotional and maybe even irrational. They are usually good with finances.

Good career ideas for Cancer are nurse, pediatrician or OB-GYN, counseling, business manager, home stager, real estate buyers' agent, archaeologist, historian, caterer, baker, nutritionist, dietitian, professional organizer, feng shui practitioner, teacher, chef, content manager, branding expert, website designer, social worker, or merchandiser.

Cancer bosses are strict about work ethics and quite devoted to whatever profession or business they are in. Employees will be rewarded for good effort in their jobs, but any slacking or bad timekeeping will be frowned upon. Cancer's own needs for financial security make the workplace a serious arena, so if you have a Cancer boss, a careful and sincere approach to all that you do will work best.

Cancer employees work for financial security mainly and, therefore, take a serious approach to their career and are very diligent. They do expect to be rewarded for their diligence with decent pay raises; if they are, they will stay in the role for a long time. Cancer will also be aiming to climb up the ladder. The biggest downside is that if a Cancer has any emotional problems in their life, they will find it hard to keep that separate from work.

Cancer coworkers are natural team players and are usually kind and caring to those they work with. However, they need a stress-free work environment—if things get chaotic, so do their emotions.

Well-known Cancer People

Nelson Mandela, Malala Yousafzai, George Michael, Missy Elliott, Michael Flatley, and Danny Glover were all born under the sign of Cancer.

LEO AT WORK

Leo loves being in the spotlight and is the royal of the zodiac, or at least that's how they expect to be treated. Leos are, however, full of heart and are passionate, playful, creative, and entertaining. As they are natural leaders, they are best suited to careers that put them in that position or doing something where they can shine their enormous light.

Examples of good Leo careers are actor, DJ, graphic designer, advertising agent, comedian, broadcaster, CEO, government worker, architect, director, event planner, media strategist, vlogger, model, product promoter, sales executive, jeweler, artist, or children's entertainer.

The Leo boss is born to lead and will let everyone know it. Leo is a good organizer and is smart about assigning tasks to a team. They are also open to new ideas but not always good at crediting those who came up with the idea. Leos generally create quite a showy environment to work in, and this can be a lot of fun if you always let them be the boss. Never try to outshine a Leo boss because they are very proud and may react like a child if thwarted.

As an employee, Leo will require a lot of ego stroking and lots of compliments and attention. They also respond well to titles and status. If you ignore them, however, they will be deeply hurt and will not respond well. They must have a position that displays their talents—when they do, their loyalty and pride in their work is immense.

If you are genuine around a Leo coworker, they will be loyal to you in the workplace. They do tend to feel they rule the workplace, though, so it's expedient to let them believe they do. When a Leo's pride and heart is hurt, they often display childlike behavior and can pout, but when a Leo is happy, they light up the room and are benevolent to everyone around them. It benefits everyone to show admiration and to compliment the Leo boss because they will return the love to all their employees.

Well-known Leo People

Madonna, Magic Johnson, Anna Paquin, Whitney Houston, and Demi Lovato were all born under the sign of Leo.

VIRGO AT WORK

Virgos are best suited to careers that utilize their critical and analytical skills. They are drawn to working with their hands, using their hand-eye coordination through technical skills. Highly organized and detail oriented, they are also drawn to careers that feel meaningful and useful to the greater good. In other words, they like to be of service to others and will pursue any career to the point of perfection.

Ideal careers for Virgo are accountant, nutritionist or dietitian, researcher, critic, data analyst, statistician, auditor, housekeeper, organizer, investigator, investor, technician, sculptor, web designer, fashion designer, 3D modeler, computer engineer, veterinarian, welder, herbalist, receptionist, psychologist, psychiatrist, bookkeeper, librarian, bank clerk, medical researcher, editor, technical writer, inspector, or engineer.

The Virgo boss will notice every detail and may have a tendency to micromanage, as they want everything to be done to their standard of perfection. They will put a lot of time into planning and forethought before making decisions, but that can sometimes mean that they don't have the perspective of the bigger picture. Virgos are their own biggest critic in all situations. Even though the Virgo boss has very high standards, they are not authoritarian, and they are excellent at crisis management because, like most earth signs, they are patient.

As an employee, Virgo lacks ego gratification and wants to serve, but they do have a sense of fairness, so they will need to be compensated fairly and they are likely to hold you to every detail of an employment contract. As Virgos tend to be worriers, their focus on those details reflects any worries they have about not being financially stable and independent. Put them in a position that utilizes their attention to detail and you and your company will be rewarded well.

Virgo coworkers are caretakers and will help more slapdash coworkers attend to the details—but that can come across as critical and nitpicking at times. They can also come across as anxious and stressed when the details aren't being taken care of. If you need an ibuprofen or some other medicine, however, your Virgo coworker will likely have it on hand because they have a keen interest in all aspects of health. They are likely to have lots of to-do lists.

Well-known Virgo People

Beyoncé, Pink, Keanu Reeves, Stephen Fry, Lily Tomlin, and Mother Teresa were all born under the sign of Virgo.

LIBRA AT WORK

Librans love peace, harmony, and balance and work best in an atmosphere that reflects that energy. They are also people-oriented and love to interact with others and form relationships, so they don't really enjoy working alone. They also enjoy any career that involves creating fairness.

Ideal careers for Libra are artist, human resources (HR) manager, mediator, diplomat, makeup artist or hairstylist, graphic designer, lawyer, matchmaker, fashion designer, guidance counselor, negotiator, event planner, nurse, business administrator, quality control officer, musician, politician, creative advertising agent, liberal arts professor, social worker, or labor relations officer.

The Libra boss would be better working in partnership than alone, but either way they will run a fair and just organization, treating everyone equally in all respects. Constant attempts to please everyone can make the Libra appear indecisive and vacillating. They don't enjoy aggressive and argumentative employees and will be impressed by those who take care of their appearance and play nice.

The Libra employee brings their calming presence into any work situation and will be a paragon of tact and diplomacy, getting along with almost everyone as long as the environment isn't loud and contentious. They are ambitious, will want deserved promotions, and, being an air, day sign, like to be given tasks that will use their intellectual capabilities.

The Libra coworker is gracious, clever, and tends to be friends with everyone. They will not take sides in heated discussions and do often take things personally, but they are likely to be kind to your face to keep a pleasant atmosphere in the workplace.

Well-known Libra People

Serena Williams, Martina Navratilova, Oscar Wilde, Will Smith, Bruno Mars, and Cardi B were all born under the sign of Libra.

SCORPIO AT WORK

Scorpio is a deep and complex sign that will work best in environments where their almost obsessive tendencies allow them to dive deeply into their work. As they are very private people, they work well alone and won't be drawn into small talk and chatting at the water cooler.

Careers that will suit a Scorpio are psychotherapist, surgeon, detective, researcher, engineer, forensics scientist, financial advisor, market analyst, bill collector, investigator, politician, political analyst, mortician, medical examiner, fertility specialist, sex therapist, chemist, shamanic healer, boudoir photographer, or undertaker.

The Scorpio boss is intense and can be intimidating, as they have a penetrative presence and can see the motivations of others, and they will use that ability to their advantage. The Scorpio boss will not immediately trust their employees but once they do, they reward deserving and talented people. Their lack of trust can create issues with delegating tasks, which can reduce productivity on the team.

The Scorpio employee keeps to themselves, is very poised, and oozes inner confidence. They are the most resourceful, single-minded, and self-motivated workers, but they are likely to be quite intimidating to both employers and employees. They are best allocated to a deep and intensive project that will allow them to stay in their zone and work alone.

The Scorpio coworker has a strong presence and insight into the psyche of their coworkers. Their natural listening abilities mean that others will share their deepest issues with the Scorpio but will learn little about them in return. Because they are so diligent, they make decent coworkers if you don't expect anything light and fluffy.

SAGITTARIUS AT WORK

Sagittarians are naturally curious, upbeat, adventurous, and best suited to a career that gives them the freedom to explore either physically or mentally. Roles where their naturally philosophical nature can shine and where they are constantly exploring new realms will also be fulfilling for them.

Sagittarians are suited to careers such as theologian, yoga teacher, publisher, travel guide, travel agent, interpreter, lawyer, judge, professor, high school teacher, ambassador, athlete (especially equestrian), entrepreneur, hotel manager, marketer, salesperson, missionary, architect, archaeologist, public relations manager, personal trainer, brand ambassador, or travel blogger.

The Sagittarius boss is fun to work for and cool to be around. They are very easygoing, and their thirst for knowledge and new experiences will give employees opportunities to expand their own field of knowledge. The one downside is the notorious Sagittarius foot-in-mouth syndrome, and they may offend those around them with their blunt and unthinking honesty.

As employees, their positive outlook is refreshing and their enthusiasm and self-confidence can rub off on other employees. They will question everything they are told, however, as they don't like being told "that's just how it's done," and their forthright honesty can be ill-received. Generally, their brilliant mind and keen approach wins out.

A Sagittarius coworker is a joy to have around if you can keep up with them. They usually have a wry sense of humor and love to make others laugh— and they also love a good debate. They tend to want to lift those around them up, however, which makes them good to work with.

Well-known Sagittarius People

Taylor Swift, Billie Jean King, Nicki Minaj, Raven-Symoné, Gianni Versace, and Jamie Foxx were all born under the sign of Sagittarius.

CAPRICORN AT WORK

Capricorns are real builders; they love to create something solid and lasting, whether that be a building, a career, or a business. They are best suited to an environment that enables them to utilize their strong work ethic and are both entrepreneurial and corporate in nature because Capricorns enjoy structure and established hierarchies.

Careers that suit the Capricorn are accountant, professional organizer, teacher, cashier, orthopedic doctor, financial planner, computer programmer, CEO, copywriter, business analyst, architect, consultant, analyst, customer service manager, legal secretary, jeweler, construction worker, electrician, human resources manager, supply chain manager, dentist, or forest management professional.

The Capricorn boss is dedicated, hardworking, and completely focused on building their career or business. You might find the Capricorn boss so focused on work that they work long hours, often to the detriment of any fun or enjoyment in their lives. The Capricorn boss can manage a team very effectively and is also good at managing difficult clients and crisis situations. Serious and hardworking team members impress the Capricorn boss.

The Capricorn employee is probably the hardest working person in the organization and will be so without any fuss and drama. As such, the Capricorn will be reserved and businesslike, follow the rules of the workplace, and doggedly climb the ladder.

As a coworker, Capricorn is likely to make sure everyone is doing their job correctly and will frown on any coworkers who are bad timekeepers or sloppy in their approach. They are also likely to be the first to agree to overtime and are very dependable, as well as generous with their time and assistance to coworkers.

Well-known Capricorn People

David Bowie, Ricky Martin, Denzel Washington, Ellen DeGeneres, Betty White, and Mary J. Blige were all born under the sign of Capricorn.

AQUARIUS AT WORK

Aquarians are the nonconformists of the zodiac and are not the best rule followers, so are best suited to an environment that utilizes their innovative and quirky nature. They are also the humanitarians of the zodiac, so if they feel their career is helping a cause of some kind they will feel more fulfilled. They often operate at a very high mental level, so they are happiest using their mind.

Aquarian careers are astrologer, astronomer, computer programmer, inventor, professor, environmental engineer, political strategist, judge, social worker, toxicologist, actor, project manager, researcher, physiotherapist, personal trainer, data analyst, environmental planner, poet, musician, electrician, x-ray technician, technical advisor, auto worker, aerospace engineer, neurologist, or hypnotherapist.

The Aquarius boss will be a reformer and innovator and will like to create new ways of doing things—they will also be open to your innovative ideas. This boss likes intellect and is distant emotionally so they will not enjoy emotional dramas in the workplace. As this person is so independent in thought and life, they are often found working alone rather than running a team.

The Aquarian employee will have a lot of friends but few deep friendships, and they will draw the team around them. They are also likely to appear absentminded and to be quite forgetful of mundane details, as their mind is constantly connecting dots about how things work in the bigger scheme of things. They are, however, conscientious, loyal, and quirky.

The Aquarius coworker is always interesting and interested in you at an intellectual level. Expect them to want to have intellectual conversations and to be really friendly. They might also try to convert you to their latest humanitarian cause. They are compassionate but will want to do something active rather than soothe others emotionally.

Alicia Keys, Alice Walker, Justin Timberlake, Harry Styles, Michael Jordan, and Oprah Winfrey were all born under the sign of Aquarius.

PISCES AT WORK

Pisceans are the dreamers and creatives of the zodiac and are best suited to careers that allow them to flow intuitively and creatively and change direction when the mood takes them. The corporate world isn't generally a fit for them unless they work in a creative capacity, because the nuts and bolts of business are not generally their forte.

Careers that suit the Pisces native are psychic, medium, artist, home decorator, social worker, nonprofit worker, counselor, nurse, physical therapist, filmmaker, musician, health educator, photographer, energy healer, caretaker, pharmacology, fiction writer, podiatrist, anesthetist, advertising executive, physicist, jailer, poet, actor, recruiter, or diver.

Piscean bosses are best when working in creative industries, as they are soft and gentle, not good at leading and giving instructions. Forceful employees will challenge the Piscean boss, but they work well if their team believes in their vision and intuitive insights.

Pisces employees must be in a career that suits their sensitive soul. Noisy, challenging, and fast-moving environments will make the Pisces employee miserable. If a Pisces individual works in a calm environment, they will work dutifully. Pisceans' naturally empathic nature makes them best suited to small teams, and they will need to protect themselves from the emotions of everyone around them.

Well-known Pisces People

Rihanna, Ellen Page, Wanda Sykes, Jon Hamm, Trevor Noah, George Harrison, and Steve Jobs were all born under the sign of Pisces.

CHAPTER TWELVE

Love According to the Zodiac

IN THIS CHAPTER, we'll take a closer look at romantic compatibility for each sign of the zodiac. While there are other important influences and factors in a person's chart that help determine romantic compatibility, this analysis provides a general guide and overview as to how each sun sign deals with love. If you want an in-depth analysis that extends beyond the sun signs, birth charts should be cast according to part 2 (see page 75). That information should be used to provide a greater understanding of each individual's strengths, their unique personalities, and how they would work together. All planets, house placements, and aspects between the two charts add detail and nuance to a compatibility reading.

Please note, there are not any "good" or "bad" pairings. Each person and sign is complex, and a combination that may have once been advised against in many astrological books and articles may actually work because of Venus and Mars connections, for example. Take this as a general guide only and think outside the box, applying the descriptions used for a sign to the person's Venus sign, for example. Also, remember to take the sign on descendant, the house placements, and the aspects between the charts into account for a deeper interpretation. We are complex human beings, and sun sign connections alone tell us only one part of the story.

ARIES IN LOVE

Aries is bold, straightforward, and forthright in love and will go after someone they desire enthusiastically. You will always know where you stand with an Aries person because of their directness. They are often the one to initiate a relationship. Their zest for life is highly appealing but can be a little overwhelming and seemingly aggressive for some gentler signs. They will never let issues fester.

- Aries and Aries are a fiery combination that is extremely passionate. Both are independent and competitive, and this can lead to lively and sometimes explosive battles, but both partners actually quite enjoy the sparring.
- Aries and Taurus are a combination of fast and passionate and slow and sensual. Aries pushes Taurus into action, whereas Taurus calms down impulsive Aries.
- Aries and Gemini are a team, with Aries taking the lead and Gemini providing the ideas that are fanned by the fire of Aries. These two have a lot of fun together.
- Aries and Cancer are a great team, with the Aries partner taking all the outer-world action and the Cancer partner keeping the home fires burning.
- Aries and Leo are another fiery combination with a lot of fun and also some explosive fights. Aries is more of the initiator, with Leo being the one who actually makes the plan real.
- Aries and Virgo are a mix of impulse and conservatism, with Aries providing excitement to liven up Virgo and Virgo bringing patience and practicality to ground Aries.

- Aries and Libra are a mix of Aries action and independence and Libra negotiation and team playing. If Aries can try to compromise a little and Libra lets Aries take the lead now and then, it will work well.
- Aries and Scorpio are a passionate combination, where the Aries openness and honesty will pierce the more private and investigative energy of Scorpio.
- Aries and Sagittarius are another fiery and adventurous combination, with only the Sagittarian lack of tact and the Aries need to dominate causing occasional issues.
- Aries and Capricorn can be a successful combination if the individual needs for independence and achievement are respected and neither tries to control the other.
- Aries and Aquarius are another bold and impulsive combination and both are likely to share a wicked sense of humor.
- Aries and Pisces can work well if Aries is aware of Piscean sensitivity and learns to compromise a little. Pisces will be endlessly loyal and flow with Aries's spontaneity.

TAURUS IN LOVE

A Taurus in love is loyal and persevering to a fault and will take their time making a commitment. When they do, however, you can be absolutely sure they mean it. Once in a relationship, their sense of family loyalty and financial stability will keep them devoted to the person they choose. If hurt, they do find it hard to forgive.

Romantic Combinations

- Taurus and Taurus are both loyal and down to earth, will enjoy all the home comforts together, and will be prepared to work to create that home.
- Taurus and Gemini are a match that will need to compromise, with a little less stubbornness and willingness to be a little more sociable from Taurus and with Gemini finding some patience and slowing down a little.
- Taurus and Cancer are both loyal and affectionate and will create an amazing home together, fulfilling each other's emotional needs.
- Taurus and Leo relationships will need a lot of compromise, as Leos are passionate and live for today and Taurus people are practical and patient and live for stability. Of course, that means that if they can compromise, they can have it all.
- Taurus and Virgo are two signs that match well, as they are both practical and responsible. Virgo brings a bit of humor to the mix and Taurus brings more sensuality.

- Taurus and Libra are both ruled by Venus—both are romantic and love luxury. If Taurus can be aware of Libra's need to be social and flirtatious and if Libra can be aware of Taurus's need for stability, they can work together well.
- Taurus and Scorpio are a case of opposites attract, and both tend to bring out the best in each other. Financially, they will be extremely stable and they are both very sensual.
- Taurus and Sagittarius can work well, as Taurus brings grounding and routine to the sometimes flighty Sagittarius and Sagittarius brings some spontaneity and optimism into the mix.
- Taurus and Capricorn are an earthy and practical combination, with Capricorn bringing ambition and humor and Taurus bringing steadfastness and providing the home base.
- Taurus and Aquarius require acceptance of differences but can work if both have similar life views. Aquarius likes to shake things up and loves intellectual exploration, whereas Taurus likes more practical and earthly things but, of course, if both can compromise, it works.
- Taurus and Pisces are a good mix, with down-to-earth practicality and stability in Taurus, while Pisces is more idealistic and compassionate. Instead

of challenging, both are likely to learn from each other.

- Taurus and Aries are a combination that either attracts or repels, with fast-moving Aries pushing Taurus into action and Taurus calming down the impulsive Aries.

GEMINI IN LOVE

Gemini in love is fast, flirtatious, and sociable and needs intellectual stimulation to the point where they often see their love as their best friend—this just means there is less emphasis on the physical side of a relationship. They are curious and fantastic listeners, which tends to charm everyone they meet.

Romantic Combinations

- Gemini and Gemini are a match that really needs some practical earth in the chart of at least one person. It will be a fun and restless intellectual relationship that can be unstable, but the friendship factor is high.
- Gemini and Cancer definitely need compromise between sociability and privacy and between the lighthearted and the sensitive. The mix of curiosity, fun, and emotional security can blend well with awareness.
- Gemini and Leo are a partnership that leads a life full of fun, affection, and probably parties. They complement each other in that Leo brings some structure and Gemini brings more flexibility.
- Gemini and Virgo are both signs ruled by Mercury and this means that both are adaptable and communicate well. Virgo brings practicality and Gemini helps Virgo lighten up a little.
- Gemini and Libra are a combination that matches well and the pair are likely to be out a lot, exploring new experiences and people and sharing ideas all the time.
- Gemini and Scorpio are a mix of depth, privacy, lightness, and openness that takes a lot of adjustment to each other. As always, it can work if Gemini allows Scorpio alone time often and if Scorpio develops a more playful side some of the time.
- Gemini and Sagittarius are a pairing that has much in common. They both like to explore intellectually and to debate, and both have great senses of humor. It's a light and playful relationship.
- Gemini and Capricorn need some mutual respect and understanding to work, as Capricorn is serious and Gemini really isn't. As always, this can work if Gemini is able to bring a sense of playfulness to Capricorn and Capricorn can bring needed grounding to Gemini.
- Gemini and Aquarius are a real meeting of the minds, and the two will

never run out of ideas or things to talk about. Both are sociable and like their independence.

- Gemini and Pisces will need compromise, as Gemini is an outgoing social butterfly and Pisces is emotional, shy, and sensitive. However, both signs are flexible, so the opportunity for each to adjust to the other's needs is there.
- Gemini and Aries are air and fire and the two elements work well together. Geminis are the mimics of the zodiac and will likely match the Aries passion, and Gemini's mind will be fueled by the fire. Lots of fun!
- Gemini and Taurus aren't the easiest of partnerships, but that makes things interesting. Taurus may find Gemini hard to keep up with and Gemini will sometimes wish Taurus would be more sociable and less stubborn, but if both can compromise, this will be a good relationship.

CANCER IN LOVE

Cancers in love are caring and sensitive, and they fall quickly and hard when they fall in love. They are likely to commit quickly and give their all to their partner, but their sensitivity can lead to emotional neediness when they don't feel loved in return. Cancer people will be the champion of their loved ones, so treat them with the love they deserve.

Compatibility Isn't Just Your Sun Sign

I give a brief overview of the compatibility of different signs here, based primarily on sun signs, but there are other ways to look at chart compatibility, such as taking into account the following elements.

Day energies tend to have an easier time understanding each other, which means fire and air signs: Aries, Gemini, Leo, Libra, Sagittarius, and Aquarius. They will generally have lively, sociable, and adventurous relationships, with the main roadblocks being practicality and emotional connection.

Similarly, night energies, Taurus, Cancer, Virgo, Scorpio, Capricorn, and Pisces, are more compatible in general and enjoy stable, productive, and bonded relationships, with the main roadblocks being lack of excitement, spontaneity, and fun.

This same principle can be applied to astrological chart connections between any planetary connections, as well as connections between the angles in the two birth charts.

Romantic Combinations

- Cancer and Cancer relationships are very loving, affectionate, and loyal, with both sensing the other's needs with ease. Both need security and can be moody, but each understands that in the other, so it's rarely a problem.
- Cancer and Leo are a very loving and passionate combination, especially if the Cancer person can remember to shower the Leo with praise as well as love and if Leo can temper any extravagance a little.
- Cancer and Virgo are a patient, grounded, and loyal match. The two signs understand each other very well and the earthy Virgo has patience with Cancer moods. Both signs are generally homebodies and conservative financially.
- Cancer and Libra pairings can have difficulties if the Cancer person doesn't understand the Libra need to be around other people and if the Libra doesn't make an effort to meet the Cancer's emotional needs. When they can do this, they can both enjoy new ways of being.
- Cancer and Scorpio are a deep and emotionally fulfilling pairing with an intuitive connection to each other. Scorpios do need more alone time than Cancer but it's rarely a problem.
- Cancer and Sagittarius partners can have difficulties, since Sagittarius is a free spirit and Cancer needs security. However, Sagittarians are usually deeply committed once they really fall in love, so that alone can mean this will work with compromises.
- Cancer and Capricorn are a good relationship in terms of loyalty and security, but the Capricorn can be a little too emotionally cool at times, so if they learn to show a little affection it will go a long way.
- Cancer and Aquarius are a mix of emotional needs and objective thought, which can be unsatisfying unless both can recognize the different needs in each other.
- Cancer and Pisces are a wonderful match because they have an almost psychic connection and are both caring and affectionate. Cancer is the better of the two with money and the two will love being together in their own world at home.
- Cancer and Aries can work well together if Aries is focused on outer-world matters while Cancer is more focused on the home and family. If the Aries partner can take time to show some affection, this relationship will work even more successfully.
- Cancer and Taurus are another loyal and affectionate pairing, and both are focused on home, family, and financial

security. They will fulfill each other's needs well.

- Cancer and Gemini are a good partnership if Cancer can be accepting of Gemini's lighthearted, fun, and flirtatious nature and if Gemini can turn that fun attention to their partner more often than to others.

LEO IN LOVE

Leo in love is exciting and openhearted as long as they are feeling loved in return. They make wonderful caring partners and are also good parents. Because they are so openhearted, however, they are easily hurt if they aren't with someone who showers them with love and attention.

Romantic Combinations

- Leo and Leo are lovely together as long as neither tries to rule over the other and they both shower each other with love, compliments, and attention. If they do that, then this is a really joyful combination.
- Leo and Virgo can be a good match, with a good mix of Leo fun and Virgo stability, as long as Virgo loosens up a little and Leo doesn't try to rule over the analytical Virgo.
- Leo and Libra will usually make an attractive and charming couple who enjoy a good social life together. If they

give each other enough attention, they will continue to be happy.

- Leo and Scorpio are two stubborn and powerful signs who both enjoy a good dramatic fight and are both loyal. Surprisingly, this often works well even though it's very intense.
- Leo and Sagittarius are a very fun and energetic partnership with some drama thrown in. Sagittarians may have to try and temper their notably blunt tongue if they don't want to bruise the Leo pride, but overall it's a great match.
- Leo and Capricorn can be a good team that grows in strength over time. Their strengths balance each other well and they each can inspire the other to reach for mutual goals.
- Leo and Aquarius are another lively and exciting partnership. Leos require a lot of attention, however, and Aquarius is often a little too detached and in their head to give enough. If Aquarius can learn to drop compliments, then this will work well.
- Leo and Pisces can be a good relationship if Leo takes the benevolent and caring ruler approach to the sensitive Pisces, rather than expecting them to stand up for themselves.
- Leo and Aries are a really good but fiery partnership and may have some big fights, but they will share plenty of

laughter, too. Aries's directness can upset Leo's tender heart at times.

- Leo and Taurus can be a wonderful pairing if the two can compromise between the Taurus's need for stability and a solid home and the Leo's outgoing passionate nature and risk-taking tendencies.

- Leo and Gemini are an exciting and lively match. Both are quite dramatic and bold and both are sociable and flirtatious, but Gemini will have to make sure some attention is kept on Leo so that their pride isn't hurt.

- Leo and Cancer are a good partnership if Cancer uses positive reinforcement with the Leo partner rather than criticism, because Leo tends to return the love and appreciation shown to them.

VIRGO IN LOVE

Virgos in love are the intellectual lovers of the zodiac and approach love cautiously and conservatively. They love to be with someone who can hold an intelligent conversation but are often drawn to a more outgoing and direct partner who will make the first move. They prefer commitment and will show their affection through acts of service rather than flowery words or lots of touch.

Romantic Combinations

- Virgo and Virgo can work if both partners commit to leaving work behind on a regular basis. The two are so in sync that it could be an "all work and no play" relationship without that commitment.

- Virgo and Libra can be a good mix of serious and frivolous if they can both be accepting of the other's approach. The good thing is that communication is a skill both excel at, so talking out differences will help.

- Virgo and Scorpio are a compatible pairing if Virgo doesn't try to logically analyze deep-feeling Scorpio and accepts that they have an innate and quiet self-confidence and spend a lot of time in silence when comfortable with a person.

- Virgo and Sagittarius are a meeting of the minds but both come from different approaches, with Virgo being more introverted and reserved and Sagittarius more outgoing and carefree. If the two can meet in the middle, this pairing will work.

- Virgo and Capricorn are two earth signs and are very well matched. The two understand and complement each other very well.

- Virgo and Aquarius will enjoy each other intellectually but Virgo may struggle with the Aquarian impracticality, though the mix of imagination and practicality can work.

- Virgo and Pisces are a challenging mix of practicality and idealistic dreaming that can only work if the two compromise, with Pisces trying to be slightly less sensitive and Virgo trying to be more so.

- Virgo and Aries will work if Virgo lets Aries be the leading light and if Aries lets Virgo take care of practical details and realizes they just enjoy doing them and aren't trying to control.

- Virgo and Taurus share a sense of responsibility and the desire to be productive and reliable, making for a generally stable and harmonious relationship, with Taurus bringing more sensuality and Virgo bringing a great sense of humor.

- Virgo and Gemini are a pairing with a high level of intellectual compatibility, with Virgo being more practical and Gemini being more sociable and sometimes frivolous. Talking things through will always help these two.

- Virgo and Cancer are a very compatible match, with both being more introverted and loyal. These two usually have a very intuitive understanding of each other.

- Virgo and Leo can work if Virgo tries not to puncture Leo's pride with criticism and Leo tries not to be domineering.

LIBRA IN LOVE

Libras love to love and be in love. They will be very affectionate and complimentary, and they love to receive the same in return. They are, however, quite picky about whom they are in relationships with and are not comfortable with partners who are insecure or not visually attractive.

Romantic Combinations

- Libra and Libra are a well-matched combination that may at times lack a little passion because it's so harmonious and based on mental compatibility.

- Libra and Scorpio have a lot of initial attraction, but Scorpio's emotional depth and Libran sociability can bring contention in a long-term relationship. The two may be a puzzle to each other, but communication can bridge the gap.

- Libra and Sagittarius are a fun and optimistic partnership with a similar sense of humor, which will help move beyond any differences in approach, such as the Sagittarius foot-in-mouth syndrome and Libran diplomacy.

- Libra and Capricorn are a stable match, with Capricorn focused on work first and Libra on relationship first, which complement each other well.

- Libra and Aquarius are a good match that has a lot in common and will be a partnership with a strong friendship element.
- Libra and Pisces are a creative and idealistic partnership that can lack the emotional connection that Pisces needs. If that can be resolved, then this can work well.
- Libra and Aries are opposite signs and have very different approaches, with Libra being all about teamwork and Aries being an individualist. If Aries can try to compromise a little and Libra lets Aries take the lead now and then, it will work well.
- Libra and Taurus share a lot of Venusian traits, as both are ruled by Venus. They share a love of harmony and luxury, for example. Both value loyalty and will be good together if Libra can tolerate the Taurus pessimism and if Taurus can know that Libra's flirtatious nature is innate.
- Libra and Gemini are an excellent partnership, with only indecision being an occasional issue for both. Both love to converse and be sociable, so they will have a lot of fun together.
- Libra and Cancer tend to have a few challenges, with Cancer needing emotional closeness and Libra being lighter and needing more social interaction. Their mutual loyalty can help them compromise well.
- Libra and Leo are a charming partnership, with both being affectionate, playful, and sociable—there is a possibility that they might have a little too much fun spending money together.
- Libra and Virgo are often seemingly at odds, with Libra being relaxed, carefree, and sociable and Virgo being productive, serious, and reserved, but this pairing actually complements and works well together.

SCORPIO IN LOVE

Scorpio in love is intense and almost obsessive, as they throw everything they have into relationships and are devoted and loyal and desire deep intimacy. They do need their alone time despite the need for such intimacy, and their feelings run so deep that they find it difficult to share them.

Romantic Combinations

- Scorpio and Scorpio are an unbelievably powerful, intense, and dramatic combination that can bring out the best or worst in each other, or both at different times. If the two merge well, then they will last for their lifetimes.
- Scorpio and Sagittarius are diametrically different and will have to work to make what can be a powerful initial attraction succeed, with Scorpio lessening their private and serious side

and Sagittarius developing some of the same.

- Scorpio and Capricorn are a well-matched pairing, as both are hard workers and reserved and value security. They each bring complementary strengths to the relationship.
- Scorpio and Aquarius are not always destined for long-term connections or harmonious ones without a lot of compromise, despite a strong attraction. The intensity of Scorpio and the detachment of Aquarius can cause conflict but with work to resolve differences, it can work.
- Scorpio and Pisces are a loyal and emotionally bonded partnership, even though Pisces doesn't always love Scorpio's tendency to be more confrontational. Both are spiritually and romantically inclined and will give to the other willingly.
- Scorpio and Aries both like to be in control, but there is a lot of passion between the two. Both are likely to enjoy the intensity and with a little communication, it can work.
- Scorpio and Taurus are in many ways perfect for each other, as Taurus's more relaxed style will complement Scorpio's intensity, and both have similar values.
- Scorpio and Gemini are an interesting mix of energies, with Scorpio being deep and Gemini liking to keep things light. Each can intrigue the other enough to keep exploring how to work together and they often do find a way to do so.
- Scorpio and Cancer are both deeply emotional, sensitive, and also possessive, which actually works here, as both feel secure in this pairing.
- Scorpio and Leo make for a very passionate and dramatic relationship but will find it hard to communicate without clashing. However, both will often enjoy this high-intensity match and that will keep them interested.
- Scorpio and Virgo are a complementary match and work well together. Both enjoy alone time and can quite easily build mutual trust.
- Scorpio and Libra speak and live at cross-purposes but have an attraction to each other in spite of that. Scorpio's privacy and intensity will confuse the lighthearted Libra, and the sociability of Libra will bring out Scorpio's possessiveness, but communication and compromise can help.

SAGITTARIUS IN LOVE

Sagittarius in love is high energy and filled with enthusiasm and fun. Sagittarius is often said to be slow to commit, but that's only because they are exploring to find someone who can keep their interest. When they do fall in love, they are usually extremely loyal. They are most attracted to those with ambition and drive.

Romantic Combinations

- Sagittarius and Sagittarius are a fun, passionate, and exploratory partnership. They both love to travel and find new experiences and do so with zest. Practicality and emotional connection can cause some issues.
- Sagittarius and Capricorn can be a good connection because the Capricorn practicality can ground the excesses of Sagittarius, while the Sagittarius partner will appreciate the ambition of Capricorn.
- Sagittarius and Aquarius are a visionary combination, with both being goal-oriented and willing to explore new ideas. This is a fun combination.
- Sagittarius and Pisces are a pairing where there is attraction, but some compromises must be made. A balance needs to be sought between the outgoing, spontaneous Sagittarius energy and the reserved and shy Pisces energy, but it can work over time.
- Sagittarius and Aries have a lot in common, and this will be a high-energy team that will enjoy activities together. Very adventurous with some volatility due to Sagittarius bluntness and the Aries need to always lead, but overall a good match.

- Sagittarius and Taurus have some challenges to overcome, as the passivity and stability of Taurus can frustrate energetic Sagittarius. However, Taurus brings grounding and routine to the sometimes flighty Sagittarius, and Sagittarius brings some spontaneity and optimism into the mix.
- Sagittarius and Gemini are a combination that can have a lot of fun together, though it can be a little unstable since both enjoy change. They both like to explore intellectually and to debate, and both have great senses of humor. It's a light and playful relationship.
- Sagittarius and Cancer have some challenges because of the mix of sensitive, emotional Cancer and blunt and fairly insensitive but fun Sagittarius. Both are quite strong-willed though, so if the attraction is there, they will tend to work things out.
- Sagittarius and Leo are a wild, passionate, and fun pairing with the potential to last a lifetime, especially if Sagittarius can rein in the brutal honesty that can hurt the Leo pride.
- Sagittarius and Virgo are a strange mix of intellectual compatibility and emotional differences, because Virgo is reserved and introverted, generally, and Sagittarius is outgoing. This match can improve with time.

- Sagittarius and Libra are a partnership full of fun and social excitement. If Libra can get over the fact that Sagittarius cares little about appearances, this will work well.
- Sagittarius and Scorpio can be challenging, because Sagittarius likes freedom and lacks the emotional intensity of Scorpio. The two will find each other fascinating, however, so differences can be worked out over time.

CAPRICORN IN LOVE

Capricorns are slow to fall in love, preferring to be friends first—but once things develop, they are stable and dedicated to creating a life with their partner. They really need someone who understands their dedication to building a secure financial foundation and, usually, a career. They are not always emotionally warm, especially early in relationships.

Compatibility by Aspect

Aspects between planets in the two astrological charts in relationships should also be taken into account. This, too, can be applied to aspects between different planets and angles and not only sun signs.

The following applies in general—note that none are good or bad, as those who challenge us in a relationship can push us to grow and develop, as long as it's a healthy challenge.

Planets in adjacent signs can have difficulty "seeing" each other, as they differ by day and night, element, and modality.

Planets in signs that are sextile to each other are harmonious, as they share day or night energy.

Planets in signs that are square to each other are more challenging, because they are always day and night energy, though they share a modality.

Planets in signs that are trine to each other are harmonious, because they share the same element and day or night energy.

Planets in signs that are inconjunct to each other are more challenging, because they are always day and night energy and they are less compatible by element and modality.

Planets in opposing signs share a modality and are both either day or night but are slightly less compatible by element, though the two are usually able to complement their opposing strengths.

Romantic Combinations

- Capricorn and Capricorn work really well together, as both share ambition, a similar work ethic, and a reserved nature. This has potential to be a stable and long-lasting relationship.
- Capricorn and Aquarius can face challenges, because Capricorn likes solid goals and plans and Aquarius is very free-spirited and prefers long-term goals without a definite plan to get there. Both are determined, however, and that can help reach a compromise.
- Capricorn and Pisces are a well-matched partnership, as Capricorn brings the practicality and Pisces brings the creative and emotional support.
- Capricorn and Aries aren't the easiest combination since Capricorn is a patient builder and loves stability and Aries likes dynamic action and is impulsive, but the pair can be a highly successful one if neither tries to control the other.
- Capricorn and Taurus are a fabulous partnership with shared values in most areas of life, and that combines Capricorn ambition and Taurus homebody tendencies well. These two are very compatible.
- Capricorn and Gemini are a mix of reserved stability and unstable sociability, which can mean differences. If the two can learn from each other without criticism, they can meet in the middle and have mutual respect and understanding.
- Capricorn and Cancer are a mixed bag. It can be a loyal partnership with a shared need for security and a stable home but Cancer needs a lot of affection and Capricorn must consciously choose to show it. Meeting in the middle is the key.
- Capricorn and Leo are both stubborn, and if the attraction is there, that means they will work at reconciling the fact that Capricorn is more reserved and pessimistic and Leo is more outgoing and optimistic, with each learning from the other.
- Capricorn and Virgo are a very grounded and reserved match with many compatibilities. Both enjoy stability and like to work hard.
- Capricorn and Libra are a partnership with differences in outlook, with Capricorn being stable, persevering, and a saver and Libra being an extrovert and a spendthrift. These differences are not irreconcilable, however.
- Capricorn and Scorpio are a good partnership where each brings out the best in the other. Both have similar ways of working and goals that will work together well.

- Capricorn and Sagittarius are a partnership where the differences can complement each other in spite of what seem to be opposite approaches, with Capricorn being cautious and Sagittarius being rash in everything they approach.

AQUARIUS IN LOVE

Aquarius in love is committed and very attentive, though not affectionate, and it takes them a while to get to the point of commitment. Aquarians are intellectuals and will want long talks about big ideas with their partner. They have an innate self-confidence, which is very attractive to others.

Romantic Combinations

- Aquarius and Aquarius are both so in their heads and detached emotionally that there is little emotional depth to the relationship. However, they may also decide they are okay with being more friends than anything else.
- Aquarius and Pisces are an unusual combination, with Aquarius being a radical thinker and Pisces being intuitive and spiritual, and that can bring challenges as the Pisces person may not have their emotional needs met. Both are deeply humanitarian, however, and that can bring them together.
- Aquarius and Aries will find each other stimulating and exciting and are a good match that looks optimistically to the future. They will share a great sense of humor.
- Aquarius and Taurus are an unlikely match with many differences, but both have staying power, which can make for a stimulating relationship that can pull them together.
- Aquarius and Gemini are a real meeting of the minds and a very dynamic pairing. Their partnership will be full of variety, fun, and a lively social life.
- Aquarius and Cancer are likely to find that the Aquarian detached emotional state doesn't fulfill the needs of the emotionally needy Cancer person. This means the two will have to communicate often about their differences to make it work long-term.
- Aquarius and Leo don't have a lot in common but that won't stop them finding this relationship stimulating and exciting, which can go a long way toward meeting in the middle.
- Aquarius and Virgo are an intellectual pairing with different strengths that can complement each other, with Virgo learning to embrace a little chaos and Aquarius learning to be a little more organized.
- Aquarius and Libra are a lovely match, with both enjoying a good social life and mental stimulation.

- Aquarius and Scorpio are a difficult and intense match that can work if the Aquarius partner learns to show some affection and the Scorpio learns to trust their partner.
- Aquarius and Sagittarius are a fun match and the two will enjoy a lot of adventures together.
- Aquarius and Capricorn are a less easy combination that can work if both use their mutual determination to iron out differences, with the main one being that Capricorn likes stability and security, and these are not priorities for the Aquarian.

PISCES IN LOVE

Pisces in love seeks a highly spiritual and intuitive connection in love. They love to love their partner and to make them feel like the most special person in the world, because they are to the Piscean. They are a gentle and openhearted soul, which can lead to them getting hurt easily by less sensitive people.

Romantic Combinations

- Pisces and Pisces are such a good match that they may never get anything practical done in their dream world of togetherness.
- Pisces and Aries can work if Aries learns some patience around their dreamy partner. If they do, Pisces will be incredibly supportive.
- Pisces and Taurus are a good match, as both share a love of romance and loyalty, with Taurus providing grounding and Pisces imagination in their lives.
- Pisces and Gemini are both very adaptable, and that may, with communication, help overcome some fairly big differences of approach. Pisces wants major emotional connection and Gemini likes to keep it light.
- Pisces and Cancer are a very loving and romantic partnership—they work together in almost psychic compatibility.
- Pisces and Leo have a lot of potential as a match if Leo soaks up the love and admiration of Pisces, avoids any desire to control them, and works to understand their sensitive nature.
- Pisces and Virgo are opposing signs and can either attract or repel. The key is integration of Pisces's dreaminess and romantic nature and the practicality of Virgo.
- Pisces and Libra are a very creative and loving match if the two can overcome the Libran need to be social and the Pisces need to stay home more.
- Pisces and Scorpio are an amazing match with a deep emotional connection, which brings a strong sense of security to these two sensitive signs.

- Pisces and Sagittarius are both very flexible and love to focus on philosophical areas of faith and belief. They will match if they can balance their introvert and extrovert natures.
- Pisces and Capricorn are a fabulous mix of common sense and dreaminess that blends well together.
- Pisces and Aquarius can work well together if they can compromise over the Aquarian's detached emotional style and Pisces's emotional sensitivity.

Astrology is an endlessly fascinating subject where there is always more to learn. With careful use of this book you will be able to understand your astrological chart in far more depth, using a more inclusive approach and language.

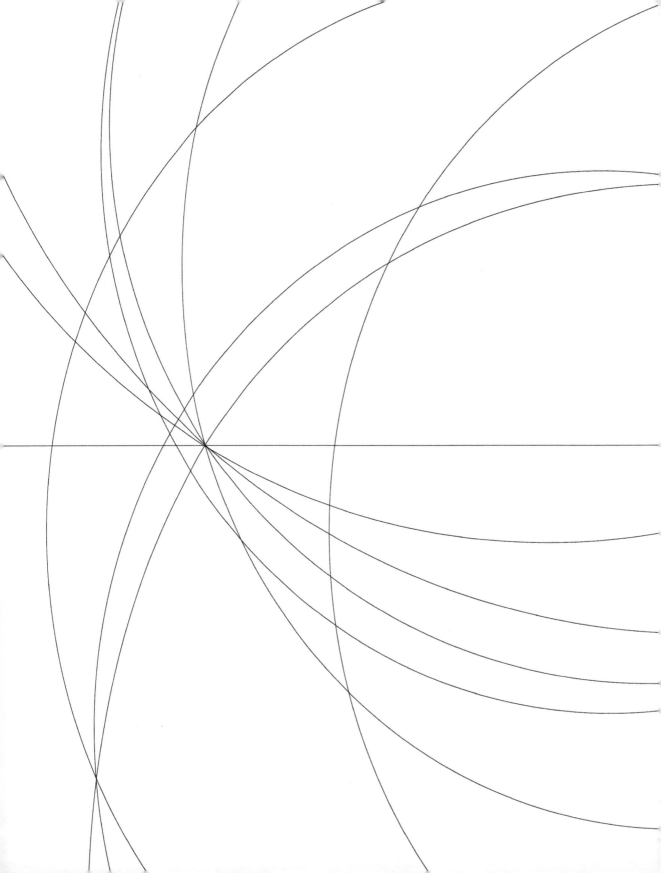

KEY TAKEAWAYS AND ASTROLOGICAL
APPENDICES

PART
4

CHAPTER THIRTEEN

Conclusion

MY HOPE IS that this book has given you a new appreciation for and a deeper understanding of key areas within astrology, as well as a new way to see astrology in nonbinary terms.

Traditionally, gendered astrological terms are based on patriarchal myths and archetypes conforming to the binary. A prime example of this is the planet Saturn. In mythology, Saturn was the god of agriculture, wealth, and generation, and Saturn's reign was depicted as a time of abundance and peace. All of these characteristics are very yin, or feminine, yet Saturn has been portrayed in much of astrology as a very masculine energy.

Another example: The symbol that represents Capricorn, the sea goat, is often portrayed as just the goat, which is more yang, and leaves out the very yin fish tail (the "sea" part of "sea goat").

If that's confusing, and it is, I suggest it is because patriarchal society has valued the masculine and devalued the feminine to the point that much of the language used by traditional interpretations of astrology has become binary and slanted. In the myths upon which our astrological interpretations are based, female goddesses were generally portrayed as evil, vengeful troublemakers or as vapid, insipid troublemakers, whereas the male gods were usually portrayed as either heroes or leaders. I am not entirely convinced the myths began that way, and there are many efforts to reclaim a more nuanced portrayal.

One thing I know for sure is that myths are stories created to represent parts of human nature. After thousands of years living under a patriarchal system, we can see how the binary is reflected in our storytelling. Our human need for certainty and definition has caused us to see finiteness and polarity where there may, in reality, be connection and integration.

It's perhaps time, therefore, to consider changing the language completely so that the portrayal of masculine as good and light and the feminine as evil and dark disappear. New language takes into account that there are good and bad qualities in both the masculine and the feminine and leaves room to define a person as more than just one or the other.

Using this new language, you can look at an astrological chart and see a more holistic view of yourself as an individual with different traits that are neither "good" nor "bad," just different.

With the advent of modern astrology, astrologers have been moving away from the use of "good" and "bad," but we need to go further and move away from using the terms "masculine" and "feminine." This opens us up to a whole new understanding of the chart.

This book, therefore, asks you to step into a more creative and imaginative space, to feel the webs of connectivity that thread through all living things, including the universe. To feel the pulse, the inhale and exhale of all that is in its multiplicity and nonlinearity. This book invites you to feel the entanglement rather than the separateness that we have approached the astrological spaces with for millennia.

The last astrological ages, Pisces and Aries, have been patriarchal in nature and have valued day energy over night. The language used in all myths and subjects like astrology has reflected that nature, valuing outgoing, "doing" energy over receptive and intuitive energy.

No one knows what the astrological age of Aquarius will bring, but Aquarius is a sign that represents entanglement and connectivity. Its symbol represents waves, perhaps quantum wave theory, waves of spirit or energy, and the sign's corulers, Saturn and Uranus, represent a curious mix of the ancient and the ultramodern, the conservative and the innovative. Aquarius is also group energy, another form of connectivity, and represents humanitarian and human rights and causes. Aquarius is visionary and futuristic.

As we stand in the doorway of the new astrological age, it is fitting that we begin to look at the language of astrology and how we approach astrology in a new way, a more inclusive and entangled way. The movements and cycles of the planets are unchanged, of course, but as I have said throughout this book, it's our perceptions and language that must change. In Greek philosophy, the concept behind *Logos* (Greek for "word") is the divine principle that permeates an orderly universe. This suggests that language has long been used to make sense of that which we don't understand. Therefore, we must now think differently and use different language to move into the new age.

This book has been your invitation to think differently and begin to feel the living universe within you, an invitation to inhabit the energies of both day and night within you. This book is for everyone.

GLOSSARY OF TERMS

AIR SIGNS: Gemini, Libra, Aquarius

ANGLES: Ascendant (ASC), descendant (DSC), midheaven (MC), and imum coeli (IC), which refer to the cusps of the first, seventh, 10th, and fourth houses, respectively

ASCENDANT (ASC): The cusp of the first house, also known as the rising sign; the point that is rising on the eastern horizon at the moment and place of birth

ASPECTS: Angular relationships between points in the natal chart

ASTEROIDS: Small rocky objects orbiting the Sun

CARDINAL SIGNS: Aries, Cancer, Libra, Capricorn

CUSP: The beginning of a house in the natal chart or where one sign ends and another begins

DECANS: Subdivisions of each astrological sign into 10° increments

DESCENDANT: Cusp of the seventh house in the natal chart, directly opposite the ascendant

DOMINION: A sign in which a planet is at its strongest

EARTH SIGNS: Taurus, Virgo, Capricorn

ECLIPTIC: An imaginary line on the sky that marks the annual path of the Sun, a projection of the Earth's orbit that also marks the line along which eclipses occur

ELEMENTS: Fire, earth, air, and water

FIRE SIGNS: Aries, Leo, Sagittarius

FIXED SIGNS: Taurus, Leo, Scorpio, Aquarius

GLYPHS: Symbols used for the astrological signs, planets, luminaries, and aspects

HEMISPHERE: A plane or line that splits the celestial sphere in half, either horizontally or vertically

HOUSES: The 12 divisions of a natal chart, each ruling over different areas of life

LUMINARIES: The Sun and the Moon

MIDHEAVEN: The cusp of the 10th house of the natal chart, the highest point in the zodiac at the moment of birth, and the most public area of the chart

MUTABLE SIGNS: Gemini, Virgo, Sagittarius, Pisces

MUTUAL RECEPTION: When two planets each occupy the sign the other rules

NODES: The two points at which the Moon, or another planet, crosses the ecliptic

ORB: Number of degrees from exact between aspect degrees

PERSONAL PLANETS: Inner planets and luminaries that have a more direct effect on the personality—the Sun, the Moon, Mercury, Venus, and Mars

PLANETARY RULERS: The planets that rule each sign

RETROGRADE: Apparent backward motion of a planet from Earth's perspective

SUN SIGN: The sign in which the Sun is at birth

TRANSIT: Ongoing movement of the planetary bodies in relationship to the horoscope

WATER SIGNS: Cancer, Scorpio, Pisces

ASTROLOGICAL TABLES

SUN TABLE

SIGN	SYMBOL	APPROX. DATES	RULING PLANETS	ENERGY
Aries	♈	Mar 21–Apr 20	Mars	Day/Inhale
Taurus	♉	Apr 21–May 20	Venus	Night/Exhale
Gemini	♊	May 21–June 20	Mercury	Day/Inhale
Cancer	♋	June 21–Jul 20	Moon	Night/Exhale
Leo	♌	Jul 21–Aug 20	Sun	Day/Inhale
Virgo	♍	Aug 21–Sept 20	Mercury	Night/Exhale
Libra	♎	Sept 21–Oct 20	Venus	Day/Inhale
Scorpio	♏	Oct 21–Nov 22	Mars—Traditional Pluto—Modern	Night/Exhale
Sagittarius	♐	Nov 21–Dec 20	Jupiter	Day/Inhale
Capricorn	♑	Dec 21–Jan 20	Saturn	Night/Exhale
Aquarius	♒	Jan 21–Feb 20	Saturn—Traditional Uranus—Modern	Day/Inhale
Pisces	♓	Feb 21–Mar 20	Jupiter—Traditional Neptune—Modern	Night/Exhale

TABLE OF MAJOR ASPECTS

PLANET IN THIS SIGN	LOOK FOR OPPOSITIONS IN...	LOOK FOR SQUARES IN...	LOOK FOR SEXTILES IN...	LOOK FOR TRINES IN...
Aries	Libra	Cancer, Capricorn	Gemini, Aquarius	Leo, Sagittarius
Taurus	Scorpio	Leo, Aquarius	Cancer, Pisces	Virgo, Capricorn
Gemini	Sagittarius	Virgo, Pisces	Leo, Aries	Libra, Aquarius
Cancer	Capricorn	Aries, Libra	Virgo, Taurus	Scorpio, Pisces
Leo	Aquarius	Taurus, Scorpio	Gemini, Libra	Aries, Sagittarius
Virgo	Pisces	Gemini, Sagittarius	Cancer, Scorpio	Taurus, Capricorn
Libra	Aries	Cancer, Capricorn	Leo, Sagittarius	Gemini, Aquarius
Scorpio	Taurus	Leo, Aquarius	Virgo, Capricorn	Cancer, Pisces
Sagittarius	Gemini	Virgo, Pisces	Libra, Aquarius	Aries, Leo
Capricorn	Cancer	Aries, Libra	Scorpio, Pisces	Taurus, Virgo
Aquarius	Leo	Taurus, Scorpio	Aries, Sagittarius	Gemini, Libra
Pisces	Virgo	Gemini, Sagittarius	Taurus, Capricorn	Cancer, Scorpio

PLANETARY TABLE

	SIGN RULED	EXALTED	DETRIMENT	FALL	DAY OR NIGHT
Sun	Leo	Aries	Aquarius	Libra	Day
Moon	Cancer	Taurus	Capricorn	Scorpio	Night
Mercury	Gemini and Virgo	Virgo	Sagittarius and Pisces	Pisces	Gemini—Day Virgo—Night
Venus	Taurus and Libra	Pisces	Aries and Scorpio	Virgo	Taurus—Night Libra—Day
Mars	Aries and Scorpio	Capricorn	Libra and Taurus	Cancer	Aries—Day Scorpio—Night
Jupiter	Sagittarius and Pisces	Cancer	Gemini and Virgo	Capricorn	Sagittarius—Day Pisces—Night
Saturn	Capricorn and Aquarius	Libra	Cancer	Aries	Capricorn—Night Aquarius—Day
Uranus	Aquarius	Scorpio	Leo	Taurus	Day
Neptune	Pisces	Cancer	Virgo	Capricorn	Night
Pluto	Scorpio	Leo	Taurus	Aquarius	Night

TABLE OF DECANS

SIGN	FIRST DECAN 0–9°	SECOND DECAN 10–19°	THIRD DECAN 20–29°
Aries	Mars/Aries	Sun/Leo	Jupiter/Sagittarius
Taurus	Venus/Taurus	Mercury/Virgo	Saturn/Capricorn
Gemini	Mercury/Gemini	Venus/Libra	Saturn and Uranus/Aquarius
Cancer	Moon/Cancer	Mars and Pluto/Scorpio	Jupiter and Neptune/Pisces
Leo	Sun/Leo	Jupiter/Sagittarius	Mars/Aries
Virgo	Mercury/Virgo	Saturn/Capricorn	Venus/Taurus
Libra	Venus/Libra	Saturn and Uranus/Aquarius	Mercury/Gemini
Scorpio	Mars and Pluto/Scorpio	Jupiter and Neptune/Pisces	Moon/Cancer
Sagittarius	Jupiter/Sagittarius	Mars/Aries	Sun/Leo
Capricorn	Saturn/Capricorn	Venus/Taurus	Mercury/Virgo
Aquarius	Saturn and Uranus/Aquarius	Mercury/Gemini	Venus/Libra
Pisces	Jupiter and Neptune/Pisces	Moon/Cancer	Mars and Pluto/Scorpio

FURTHER READING

ASTROLOGY FOR THE SOUL by Jan Spiller (Bantam, 2009)

THE SECRET LANGUAGE OF BIRTHDAYS: *Your Complete Personology Guide for Each Day of the Year* by Gary Goldschneider and Joost Elffers (Avery, 2013)

THE INNER SKY: *How to Make Wiser Choices for a More Fulfilling Life* by Steven Forrest (Seven Paws Press, 2012)

MODERN ASTROLOGY: *Harness the Stars to Discover Your Soul's True Purpose* by Louise Edington (Althea Press, 2018)

MYSTERIES OF THE DARK MOON: *The Healing Power of the Dark Goddess* by Demetra George (Harper Collins, 1992)

To create a free natal chart online:

ALABE.COM/FREECHART

ASTRO.CAFEASTROLOGY.COM/NATAL.PHP

ASTRO.COM

To find your ascendant:

ASTRO.COM

Free astrology apps:

TIME NOMAD

TIMEPASSAGES

INDEX

ABOUT THE AUTHOR

LOUISE EDINGTON has been studying and practicing astrology for 30 years and writes daily astrology posts that guide readers through their lives. She enjoys all aspects of professional astrology, but her main passion is helping clients regain a deep connection with the cycles of the universe so that they find deep acceptance and self-awareness. Louise provides astrological counseling, astrology classes, and writing and also offers support through a Cosmic Membership Community. You can learn more about her services at louiseedington.com. Louise's first book, *Modern Astrology: Harness the Stars to Discover Your Soul's True Purpose,* is available on Amazon.

NOTES

NOTES

NOTES

NOTES

NOTES

NOTES

NOTES

NOTES

NOTES

NOTES

NOTES